What People Are Saying About
ROBERT L. DILENSCHNEIDER
and His Books

DECISIONS
Practical Advice from 23 Men and Women Who Shaped the World

"Upgrade your daily decisions with the wisdom of two dozen renowned influencers who changed history."
—**Mehmet Oz, MD,** Emmy Award–winning host of
The Dr. Oz Show

"Sound advice wrapped in often little-known stories of a broad range of people from JFK to Ignaz Semmelweis. Fun to read and sound."
—**Fay Vincent,** former commissioner of
Major League Baseball

"This supremely thoughtful book will help any reader to think more clearly about the decisions they face and, crucially, about the contexts in which those decisions must be made."
—**Bill Emmott,** former editor in chief, *The Economist*

"*Decisions* is a truly inspiring book about how to become a leader. Highly recommended!!"
—**Douglas Brinkley,** *New York Times* bestselling author of
American Moonshot: John F. Kennedy and the Great Space Race

"The best decision you will make today is to read and learn from this array of bold thinkers. Bob Dilenschneider offers remarkable insights that give new perspectives on our own decisions, large or small."
—**Harvey Mackay,** author of the #1 *New York Times* bestseller *Swim with the Sharks* '

D1621781

THE CRITICAL FIRST YEARS
OF YOUR PROFESSIONAL LIFE

"Dilenschneider knows that the first fourteen years of your professional life, properly managed, will propel you forward for the rest of your career. Whether the economy is weak or strong, he will help you navigate through the changing tides."
—Maria Bartiromo, host of *Mornings with Maria*

"Practical advice on how young people can take charge of their careers and develop independently both the skills required to excel in any environment and the savvy to know when to move on."
—Norman R. Augustine, former Chairman and CEO of Lockheed Martin Corporation

"An insightful, idea-laden, practical guide that will be valuable to young professionals seeking to advance their on-the-job lives."
—Stephen A. Greyser, Richard P. Chapman Professor of Business Administration, Emeritus, Harvard Business School

"This book is for anyone who wishes to make his or her mark in the business world. Bob Dilenschneider . . . shares strategic advice and years of tested experience with younger people who are just bringing their unpolished talents to the marketplace."
—Rev. Theodore M. Hesburgh, President Emeritus, University of Notre Dame

"This book should be essential reading for young people starting out on a business career."
—Henry Kaufman, Henry Kaufman & Company

Books by
ROBERT L. DILENSCHNEIDER

Nailing It★

Decisions★

The Critical First Years of Your Professional Life★

50 Plus!★

The Critical 2nd Phase of Your Professional Life

Power and Influence

Civility in America

Public Relations Handbook

A Briefing for Leaders

The AMA Handbook of Public Relations

A Time for Heroes

Values for a New Generation

On Power

The Men of St. Charles

The Corporate Communications Bible

The Hero's Way

★Available from Kensington Publishing Corp.

NAILING IT

HOW HISTORY'S AWESOME TWENTYSOMETHINGS GOT IT TOGETHER

ROBERT L. DILENSCHNEIDER

Foreword by

U.S. Ambassador Donald Blinken

CITADEL PRESS
Kensington Publishing Corp.
www.kensingtonbooks.com

CITADEL PRESS BOOKS are published by

Kensington Publishing Corp.
119 West 40th Street
New York, NY 10018

All Kensington titles, imprints, and distributed lines are available at special quantity discounts for bulk purchases for sales promotions, premiums, fund-raising, educational, or institutional use.

Special book excerpts or customized printings can also be created to fit specific needs. For details, write or phone the office of the Kensington sales manager: Kensington Publishing Corp., 119 West 40th Street, New York, NY 10018, attn: Sales Department; phone 1-800-221-2647.

ISBN: 978-0-8065-4175-4

First Citadel trade paperback printing: January 2022

10 9 8 7 6 5 4 3 2 1

Printed in the United States of America

Electronic edition:

ISBN: 978-0-8065-4176-1 (e-book)

To ROBERT LAIRD:

*A man of style and substance who has quietly
had a positive impact on his country and the world.*

CONTENTS

FOREWORD

by U.S. Ambassador Donald Blinken

Biographies normally focus on the achievements of individuals—their victories in battle, scientific innovations, political triumphs, artistic breakthroughs—as well as the obstacles they faced and the defeats they suffered on the road to success.

In this book, Robert Dilenschneider, the widely respected author and communications consultant, offers a fresh way at looking at the factors that contributed to the reputations of twenty-five outstanding men and women. He concentrates in particular on their lives when they were 25 years old, or thereabouts—mature enough to strike out on their own, in some cases certain of what their careers would be, in several other cases not so certain at all. He takes a thorough look at the things that helped them make their game-changing decisions: education, parental guidance, the influence of contemporaries, external events in the world, and many other factors.

Specifically, he focuses on a carefully selected group of twenty-five landmark figures from three perspectives:

- Where they were in life at age 25 (or so)
- What did they go on to do that would put them in the history books

- How did they do it—what were the turning points, what were the adversities they had to overcome, what were the unique personal traits that enabled them to persevere

In other words, he offers a fresh look at the sources of achievement—not simply the results.

This book was born out of Bob Dilenschneider's concern about how demoralizing it is for many young people to consider their futures. Young people who believe that their education may be useless and that their career opportunities have fallen apart before they have even started out. The book is written to demonstrate that many of history's most accomplished people were in similar situations when they were at about the same stage in life. Some, without knowing it, were already on the path to success. Some had fallen off that path and had to find it again. Some didn't even know that for them there was a path. Yet in the end, all of them found their way and made memorable contributions.

And so, this book is aimed at members of the generation that is coming of age right now. But it is also for their elders—the parents and other significant figures in their lives who care about them and their futures. After all, the responsibility of older generations to help the young people of the twenty-first century cannot be overstated.

Reading this book reminded me of British philosopher Isaiah Berlin's often-quoted observation about people falling into two groups. Some, he said, are foxes. Others are hedgehogs. The fox knows many things. The hedgehog knows one, but he knows it extremely well.

The readers of this fascinating book can draw their own conclusions about what category they belong in. But whatever their feeling, they will find within these pages plenty of inspiration for their own paths forward.

INTRODUCTION

This book tells the stories of twenty-five men and women from around the globe who started with modest means and who helped change the world.

The idea is to inspire young people and help them recognize that they can make a difference. For the more mature this book offers a snapshot of history in the making.

Life is different because of the twenty-five treated in these vignettes.

My hope is that knowing where these people were in their lives at that age—whether their acts were together, or not—will be informative and encouraging. Their stories offer some perspective on what young people are experiencing now. For most of us at 25 or so, the future is at least unknown, perhaps a bit daunting. It does not have to be this way. No matter where you are on the stage of life, the stories of these people should enlighten you. You could say that they nailed it. And you can nail it too.

ALBERT EINSTEIN is the quintessential example of someone whose prospects seemed hopeless in his mid-twenties. Doesn't everyone know that the genius and future Nobel laureate was stuck in a drab desk job in the Swiss patent office? What many people don't realize—though they will, when they read his story—is that this was an intensely creative time for the young physicist. Working in a seemingly mindless job (he actually liked it) gave his imagination free rein. He had the time and headspace he needed to produce and publish his groundbreaking theories.

At the other end of the spectrum is OTHMAR AMMANN, a contemporary of Einstein's (they even attended the same prestigious Swiss university). By his mid-twenties, his path was set. He had acquired the education and the novice experience he needed to develop his unparalleled career building famous bridges around the world. With determination, he set one foot in front of the other toward his goal.

STEVE JOBS and JEAN-MICHEL BASQUIAT are also at opposite ends of a spectrum. Both were self-made in very interesting ways. Both were at the top of their game at or before age 25—Jobs having made his first of millions of dollars and Basquiat being recognized as a world-class artist. But though Jobs had another half a lifetime to continue to succeed, Basquiat would soon be dead from a drug overdose.

Many of the people profiled in this book had rocky starts in life, often close to tragic. HELEN KELLER, deaf and blind. EDITH PIAF and COCO CHANEL abandoned as children. MAYA ANGELOU molested and raped. MARY SHELLEY widowed young. AUDREY HEPBURN, World War II privations. Yet these women gave the world an abundance of grace, art, literature, music, beauty, civil rights activism, and philanthropy.

"Aha moments" happened for two of our people in their mid-twenties. SALLY RIDE was well on her way to a good academic career when she happened to read about NASA accepting its first class of female astronaut candidates—the rest is history. HONORÉ DAUMIER immediately grasped the implication of combining the relatively new art form of lithography with political satire.

Two people stepped into the roles that were expected of them: WOLFGANG AMADEUS MOZART, a child prodigy of a musician who was molded by his father, and ROBERTO MARINHO, who at an early age inherited the Brazilian newspaper his father had founded. Mozart enjoyed early success, then lost it, then found success again—and died in his mid-thirties. Marinho enjoyed continued success and influence over a long life span.

On the other hand, two of the people in this book resisted the roles that others assigned them: AKIO MORITA and RITA LEVI-MONTALCINI. Morita was expected to take over his family's centuries-old business, following the example of fifteen generations of his predecessors. Levi-Montalcini was supposed to become a traditional wife and mother, not even going to college; certainly not becoming a doctor. Carving their own paths, Morita founded Sony and Levi-Montalcini won a Nobel in medicine (and became neither a wife nor a mother).

Focus, sometimes bordering on obsession, marks the stories of GOLDA MEIR, I. M. PEI, MARIA TALLCHIEF, and RUDOLF NUREYEV. Meir became dedicated to Zionism as a young teenager and devoted all her energies from then on, to the end of her life, to Israel. Pei, knowing he wanted to be an architect, chafed at the classical education that was necessary—yet persisted at it and then went on to break the mold and express his own vision around the world. Tallchief and Nureyev were highly trained ballet dancers who took risks to break molds—Tallchief being the first American and Native American prima ballerina and Nureyev the first Soviet artist to defect to the West during the Cold War.

BRANCH RICKEY and JACKIE ROBINSON present lessons in picking up in the face of failure and discrimination, and then moving ahead into success. Men of different generations, men of different races and backgrounds, they hold their place in history because of a singular event: breaking Major League Baseball's so-called color line. And they were also darn good at baseball, Rickey at the business end and Robinson as a player.

CHRISTA MCAULIFFE gives us the example of a woman who moved smoothly through her twenties because she was already what she had always wanted to be: a wife, a mother, and a teacher. When opportunity—an unexpected one, yet perfectly fitting her skill-set—presented itself in her middle age, she embraced it. She became NASA's first "ordinary citizen" astronaut; as we all know, her goal to present lesson plans from space ended when the *Challenger* exploded.

On the other hand, ELIZABETH KENNY gives us the example of a woman who had no idea what she wanted to be, or what she could do, until a disparate set of circumstances came together in her thirties. She then forged ahead, in spite of enormous bias and terrible criticism, to make a unique contribution to health care; the modern feminist expression, "nevertheless, she persisted," fits her to a T.

Finally, ULYSSES S. GRANT—a military man and a politician—is a singularly sympathetic figure, whose story can give anyone hope. He came from nothing, was on the verge of making something of himself at age 26, and lost his way by age 32. It took him almost a decade to regain his footing. With his forties came accomplishments. And then, once again, he stumbled *and* recovered. How human!

My hope is that the stories in this book will help every reader realize that there are many paths forward. Some paths are smooth, while others are rocky. Some are routine and quotidian, others are novel. Some seem to go around in circles. Some require daring, bravery, and rebellion. Whether you are a young person, or someone who loves a young person and wants to help him or her—or whether you are an "old" person taking stock of things—know that each path is unique, just as each person is unique. Just as *you* are unique.

I

WOLFGANG AMADEUS MOZART
(Austria)

UNEMPLOYED! YOU WERE OFF TO A GOOD START in your career, even enjoying some early recognition. And then you were fired and had to start over. Sound familiar?

That's what happened to Wolfgang Amadeus Mozart, who was 25 when he lost his job. He picked himself up and started over successfully, only to taste failure and success again and again. It was a relentless cycle. Then he died. He was 35.

Lest this is all too demoralizing, consider that the man I just described is known and admired today, some 250 years after his time, as possibly the greatest composer who ever lived. If anything earthly can be considered eternal, it is Mozart's music.

Despite the many setbacks, as the great twentieth-century composer Aaron Copland wrote: "What we expect to find in Mozart is perfection in whatever medium he chose to work."

What a fascinating person Mozart was!

- A product of his times—he was born and died in the waning years of the Holy Roman Empire, which controlled and directed every aspect of Western European life for a millennium.
- A child prodigy, mastering many instruments (except the

trumpet, whose sound frightened him), composing music and performing in public—to acclaim—starting at age 6.

- A son both dutiful and rebellious to a father who "home-schooled" him and supported his career, and who later opposed his marriage.
- A prolific adult, composing with speed and excellence in every musical genre: concertos, operas, symphonies, choral and chamber music, sonatas.
- A popular concertizer and conductor.
- A denizen of royal and religious settings who knew how to align with powerful patrons.
- An ambitious and energetic man subject to depression, perhaps bipolar.
- A rebel, a spendthrift, a figure of tragedy who endured the deaths of many family members.

And with all this, what a relatable person he was! Let's consider his life, his work, and his gifts to the world.

Mozart was born in Salzburg, Austria, on January 27, 1756. He was the youngest child of seven, five of whom had died in infancy. His mother Anna Maria's labor was difficult. Her baby was delicate and not expected to live. As an adult, he was robust neither in health nor appearance; various sicknesses plagued him, and he had an almost child-like stature.

His surviving sister Maria Anna (familiarly called Nannerl) was his elder by five years. They grew up in a happy home, as far as is known, and both excelled musically at a young age. In particular, little Wolfgang's precocity as a performer and a composer was soon apparent. This raises interesting nature-versus-nurture questions. Their father Leopold was himself a talented and well-connected professional musician. He tutored the children in music (and all academic studies as well; there was no formal education) and traveled with both of them to music venues throughout Europe.

Mozart suffered from eighteen serious illnesses during his life, according to Dr. Peter Davies, an Australian gastroenterologist with numerous books to his credit about the health of both Mozart and Beethoven. Smallpox, typhoid fever, quinsy, rheumatic fever, tonsillitis, and jaundice plagued Mozart, as did repeated respiratory infections. In a 1983 article in the *Journal of the Royal Society of Medicine*, Dr. Davies pointed out that the frequent long trips during which young Wolfgang and Nannerl were "paraded and exhibited" around Europe led them to be "exposed to the many endemic and epidemic diseases of those times. The journeys were usually undertaken in uncomfortable carriages, amidst all extremes of weather and often in unsatisfactory accommodation." Mozart's trips as an adult were undoubtedly also in such "uncomfortable" and "unsatisfactory" conditions. It's amazing he lived to age 35.

Leopold was employed as a concertmaster within the Salzburg royal court, which, in the political power structure of the Holy Roman Empire (800–1806), was also a center of Christianity and artistic endeavor. Prince-archbishops were Leopold's patrons and one of them, Hieronymus von Colloredo, became his son's benefactor as well.

In 1773, when Wolfgang was 17, he and his father had just concluded a four-year series of appearances throughout Italy, designed to showcase the younger man's abilities as performer and composer. Nannerl, alas, stayed home in Salzburg with her mother; according to the conventions of the time, it was no longer appropriate for the maturing young woman to perform in public.

Archbishop von Colloredo took notice and hired Wolfgang as an assistant concertmaster. With free rein to exercise his musicality, Mozart was in a position that would have been enviable at any age—but at age 17, truly remarkable. Four remarkable and productive years followed.

Yet, as often happens, professional and physical restlessness set in, no doubt enhanced by a certain amount of immaturity. In 1777, Mozart decided to leave Salzburg. While continuing to be employed by the archbishop, he set out to "explore other options" in Germany and France. Traveling about with his mother Anna Maria, he did not find what he thought he was looking for and began running short of money. When, tragically, his mother died while they were still traveling, his quest was over. He returned to Salzburg in 1779 at age 23 in what must have been a chastened state.

Thanks to his father's efforts, Wolfgang gained a position as a court organist, while still composing and working for von Colloredo. In fact, he wrote music ceaselessly throughout his life, with over six hundred works bearing his name. He seldom revised his work; it sprang in almost finished form directly from his imagination.

In 1781, he was summoned to accompany the archbishop to Vienna, for ceremonies marking the ascension of Joseph II to the Austrian throne as emperor. A possibly career-ending falling-out took place between employer and employee—does this sound familiar?—and Mozart embarked on the uncertain life of a freelancer. He was now 25.

An academic analysis of Mozart's career assigns it three stages: early (1761–72, age 5–16), middle (1772–81, age 16–25), and late (1781–91, age 25 to death at 35). His best-known work was produced in the late stage, but there was never a hiatus in his output. Ultimately, Mozart was responsible for 21 stage and opera works, 15 Masses, over 50 symphonies, 25 piano concertos, 12 violin concertos, 27 concert arias, 17 piano sonatas, 26 compositions for string quartets—and his oeuvre includes over 400 other pieces.

★ ★ ★

Let's pause here and think about why Mozart's music is so captivating and enduring. I'm no musicologist, but I know beauty when I hear it. Mozart's music *is* beauty. For you, as for me, that may be enough. Musicologists and musical greats, though, can help us understand the underpinning of that beauty.

"Pure thinking in sound" is the judgment of Paul Grabbe, author of a tiny little volume—just the right size to slip into a pocket and take to the concert hall—that I have long possessed called *The Story of One Hundred Symphonic Favorites*. (Unfortunately, I have lost the companion volume on opera.) Grabbe, who wrote in 1940, went on to praise Mozart's oeuvre for its distinctive style, brightness, and grace, and he absolutely rejected the popular concept of Mozart as a composer of "enchanted trivialities."

Leonard Bernstein, of course, transcended musicology and inhabited his own realm of musical genius as conductor, composer, and New York Philharmonic icon. One of his many endeavors was, in 1959, a series of television productions aimed at "bridging the gulf between composer and concert-going public." The scripts are included in his book *The Infinite Variety of Music,* first published in 1966. In "The Ageless Mozart" script, he too scoffed at the notion that his eighteenth-century predecessor represented only "aristocratic delicacy and nothing more." Mozart's genius "was a universal one," Bernstein wrote. "He captured not only the feel and smell and spirit of his age but also the spirit of . . . all epochs."

Bernstein was equally firm in dismissing the cavil that Mozart was a mere recycler of musical themes. He agrees that Mozart's musical vocabulary was limited by the conventions of his time—a fact that is, of course, true of all composers—but insists that invention "was his middle name." "The wonder is not that he used conventional formulas, but that, using them, he was able to create such amazing variety."

★ ★ ★

After finally parting company with Archbishop von Colloredo, Mozart stayed in Vienna, moving into a household whose daughter Constanze he promptly fell in love with. Despite Leopold's initial opposition, thought to be rooted in his fear that domesticity would sap his son's creativity and derail his career, Wolfgang and Constanze married in 1782. He was 26 and she was 18. In the early years of the marriage, Mozart's freelance career took off. His father's fears seemed unfounded. Performing concerts and publishing his music became financially rewarding. His popularity soared.

For a time, personal happiness accompanied professional success. But, as we know and as Mozart experienced, all wheels go 'round and 'round.

In a terrible echo of Wolfgang's parents' experience, Constanze bore six children, though she suffered terribly through her pregnancies and only two babies survived infancy. Constanze's continuing ill health—coupled with her husband's bouts of illness—necessitated many unavoidable expenses. Avoidable expenses were also incurred. A middle-class man, Mozart tried to emulate the aristocrats who were his audiences. The young couple began to live beyond their means.

By the mid-1780s, Mozart was again seeking "steady" employment through a court appointment. A vigorous rivalry sprung up between him and Antonio Salieri, a Venetian composer prominent in Vienna. (Remember that name.) At this time of anxiety and insecurity, though, artistic creativity continued unabated, with Mozart collaborating with the Venetian composer and poet Lorenzo Da Ponte on the stunning operas *Le Nozze di Figaro* ("The Marriage of Figaro") and *Don Giovanni*.

Providentially, Emperor Joseph II, whose 1781 coronation had been the occasion of Mozart's falling-out with his first patron, in 1787 named Mozart "chamber composer." It was a royal honor, though it was better for his reputation than for his finances. It provided ample time for Mozart to continue his freelance career, which produced a third opera with Da Ponte, *Così Fan Tutte* ("Thus Are They [Women] All").

By the end of the decade, Mozart, whose work never flagged in output or quality, was in dire financial straits. And then the wheel turned yet again and Phoenix-like, he seemed to be on the rise. In May 1789 came the first performance of Symphony no. 41 in C major, the one that has earned the nickname "Jupiter" for its magisterial magnificence.

Once again, though only briefly, Mozart was in high demand for public appearances, and was earning financial support from new patrons. And his compositional productivity never ceased. In mid-1791 came *Die Zauberflöte* ("The Magic Flute"), one of the best known of his twenty-plus operas.

And somehow, it all became too much, as can happen with any of us. Affected by rapid cycles of creation and reinvention, his physical, mental, and emotional health failed drastically. Leaving one of his greatest works, the *Requiem*, unfinished, Mozart died in Vienna on December 5, 1791, at age 35. Young Constanze (she was 27 when she was widowed) carried on. She resolved the family's debts by writing two biographies of her husband; she eventually married a Danish diplomat.

Remember Antonio Salieri? It was rumored that he fatally poisoned Mozart, their rivalry was so bitter. This rumor was fruitful for at least four other artists. It became the basis for story lines in an 1832 play by Alexander Pushkin and an 1897 one-act opera by Nikolai Rimsky-Korsakov (both works entitled *Mozart and Salieri*). And of course, there was *Amadeus* the 1979 play by Peter Shaffer that he adapted into the 1984 film directed by Milos Forman. But in truth, it was not obvious what killed Mozart, and the question remains fascinating for fans of Mozart. As many as one hundred possible causes have been put forward, including complications from what we now call "pre-existing conditions," the after-effects of illnesses that he had suffered throughout his brief life.

Earlier, I said that Mozart was both fascinating and relatable. A genius, indeed, but so human. Each time he was lost, it's likely that he wondered, as we all do, if he would ever find his way again, or be found.

Because of his profound influence and enduring contributions to the canon of Western classical music, Mozart lays claim to the title of one of the greatest composers of all time. But with six hundred plus works to his credit, how can anyone begin to appreciate his breadth and depth? Where to start listening?

I sought input from the website of my go-to classical music station, New York City's WQXR, which points out that there are an estimated ten thousand of his recordings in print. This makes building a Mozart library a daunting task. But an annotated list of "The 20 Essential Mozart Recordings" can be found on www.wqxr.org—along with the actual recordings themselves accessible via Spotify. *That's* a good place to start listening.

2

MARY SHELLEY
(United Kingdom)

MARY SHELLEY HAS NEVER LEFT US, because her work keeps her alive for us. Almost two centuries after she lived and wrote, Mary Shelley retains a firm grip on the world's imagination.

This is largely because of her masterpiece, *Frankenstein*, with its nightmarish vision of humanity gone awry. She wrote the book in her late teens, amidst tremendous turmoil in her life. The recent two hundredth anniversary of its publication, along with the re-discovery of her plague-centered novel *The Last Man* because of the worldwide coronavirus pandemic, has brought renewed popular, biographical, and scholarly attention. Mary Shelley's visibility and reputation are sky-high.

Much of that attention has come from women, I have noticed. I think that is because her story resounds with women in a way that men don't quite get. I'll do my best to honor her story.

It should be evident by now that I enjoy history and biography. The reason is simple. It is not voyeurism. It has to do with helping me understand other people and what they do. Understanding others is vital for every relationship in life—spouses, friends, family members, voters, customers, colleagues—be they casual, sustained, positive, or negative. I want to understand people I meet in life, as well as historical figures who have shaped our country and the world. Mary Shelley is a very compelling person.

By the age of 24, almost 25, Mary Wollstonecraft Godwin Shelley had not only written a book of great renown, but she had also suffered mightily, more than most young women. Lest you think I am being melodramatic, consider this bare-bones catalog of tragedy, scandal, loss, separation, and difficulty. I would wish none of these events on anyone:

Born in 1797, Mary was 10 days old when her mother died; a toddler when her father remarried, to "a woman I shudder to think of," as Mary later said; 15 when she was sent away by her father and her stepmother to live with another family; 16 when she was forced to return; 17 years old when she ran away with a married-with-kids man, by whom she became pregnant; 18 when the prematurely born baby died; 19 when her lover's pregnant wife committed suicide, and she and her lover married; 24 when her husband was killed. By then, she had given birth to three more children, only one of whom survived into adulthood, and had lost another to miscarriage. She had spent seven years at the unstable center of a louche and ever-shifting cast of people who toyed with fame, financial insecurity, and personal entanglements of all kinds.

By the age of 25, though, it was also evident that Mary Shelley was leading a life that offered more than pathos. Capable of enduring feats of literary creativity, she was one of the earliest writers of both science fiction and gothic horror, with themes that remain astonishingly fresh. She was also muse and talented editor for the work of her lover/husband, the poet Percy Bysshe Shelley.

Throughout her entire and relatively short life—which ended in 1851 at age 54—Mary Shelley wrote and published prolifically. Her output included 24 short stories, 21 articles and reviews, 18 poems, 7 novels, 5 biographies, 3 children's books (including one co-authored with Percy), 2 travel narratives, and dozens of journals, letters, fragments, and drafts. She was well regarded.

After her death, though, and until recent years, Mary's own literary reputation was largely overshadowed by her husband's, which she helped burnish during his life. Editing and publishing Percy's work was an especially important endeavor after his death when she needed to support herself and her surviving child.

Let's go back to Mary Shelley's origins, fill in some details, and consider the first half of her life. You may find her story as disturbing as I do. But consider whether its sadness provided the fertile ground for her genius to flourish. A worthy trade-off?

She was born on August 30, 1797, in England at a time when many conventions of life were being examined and often up-ended in the pursuit of freedoms of all kinds. Many of these conventions involved the most intimate of relationships: the roles and rights of women and men, of wives and husbands, of mothers and fathers; the responsibilities of parents, especially fathers, toward children, who generally had no rights at all; the necessity of marriage versus the desirability of "free love," to name just a few.

The year 1797 was also the cusp of two major intellectual eras or movements—the Age of Enlightenment when science and reason were dominant, and the Romantic Era when the expression of human and natural emotion, especially through the visual, musical, and literary arts, became more important.

Mary Wollstonecraft Shelley's parents played no small part in these huge cultural shifts. Under any circumstances, the effects on their daughter would have been significant. Add to that her unique set of traumas—and her unique talents—and the result is fascinating.

She was named for her mother, the feminist philosopher and activist Mary Wollstonecraft, famous for writing the controver-

sial treatise *A Vindication of the Rights of Women* in 1792. Her father was the noted political philosopher, writer and publisher
William Godwin; his work espoused controversial theories such
as anarchy and utilitarianism.

When Mary's parents met and fell in love, finding that they
had conceived, they debated whether marriage was necessary
for the legitimacy of the new child. Mary Wollstonecraft already had a 3-year-old daughter from an affair, so the question
of legitimacy was more than academic. Eventually the answer
was "Yes." This decision caused fury among William's follow-
ers because he had previously advocated for the abolition of
marriage. Interestingly, husband and wife continued to keep
separate households. Mary Wollstonecraft was 38 and William
41, mature people.

The wedding took place just a few months before baby
Mary's birth at home with a midwife in attendance, customary
at that time. Complications ensued that necessitated calling in a
physician, who—as was also customary at this time—treated the
new mother without washing his hands. The result was puerperal fever ("childbed fever"), which killed mother Mary ten
days later. She was able to nurse her infant briefly before the in-
fection coursing through her body made it too dangerous to do
so; tiny and frail Mary was removed to the care of a wet nurse.
William contemplated his future as a father of a daughter and a
stepdaughter; biographers said he was distraught.

Too late to help Mary Wollstonecraft and countless other
women, in 1847 the Hungarian physician and scientist Ignaz
Semmelweis made the connection between germ-laden
hands and puerperal fever. His revolutionary and simple pre-
scription of . . . handwashing . . . for anyone attending to birth-
ing mothers expanded into all aspects of medical care and
personal hygiene.

Despite this terrible loss, William Godwin seemed able to offer a secure life for the young girls. He kept their mother's memory alive for both of them, not for maudlin reasons but from a sense of love and appreciation. Because of his status as a public intellectual, his home was enlivened by visitors such as Samuel Coleridge and William Wordsworth. He doted on little Mary especially. He taught her "letters" by tracing her fingers over the carvings on her mother's gravestone and allowed her free rein among the books in his library, both early literary influences. His remarriage, when she was 4 years old, was a turning point, another loss for the girl.

Godwin's new wife was Mary Jane Clairmont, a neighbor known as "the Widow," though technically she was not a widow, having never been married. A journalist later described her as "a vulgar and worldly woman" who was, strange as it might seem for a wife to William, "rather inclined to boast of her total ignorance of philosophy."

These traits did not deter the new couple from establishing a publishing company called the Juvenile Library that existed, not always profitably, for decades; there was a related bookstore as well. The company handled diverse works that included William's own writing (some of it, children's stories under a pseudonym so as not to offend parents who opposed his political leanings), a book by a pupil of Mary Wollstonecraft, and the English translation of *The Swiss Family Robinson*. One of their titles, Charles and Mary Lamb's *Tales from Shakespeare*, became a classic for children that has never been out of print.

Regardless of her marital status, the Widow already had a son and a daughter; she and William would soon have a son together. Blended now into the household were five children, semi-related to each other, none of them with the same two parents.

One of the children—Mary—grew deeply unhappy. The affection, or at least the attention, of her only parent had been diverted. Her new stepmother, never an easy or pleasant woman, may have been jealous of the previous close relationship between William and Mary. Even the literate environment provided by the home library, the publishing company, and the bookstore did not seem to soothe Mary. Eventually, when the girl was barely in her teens, William and the Widow sent her away to live with a family in Scotland whom they had never met but who were known to admire Godwin. Mary thrived there. It was a sorrow for her to be called back to England a year later and put to work in the family bookstore.

As I have already indicated, so much of Mary Shelley's entire life was troubling: psychologically challenging and full of instability. Today we would say she suffered from "attachment disorder," that she had "abandonment issues." At the very beginning of her existence, she lost her mother, an individual and an archetype. At the age of 4, she lost her father—also both an individual and an archetype—to a relationship that, while it may have been appropriate for the adults involved, was hard for her, a child, to accept because it supplanted her. A favored child who had been her father's focus, she became just one of many people in a crowded household. Within a few years, she was ejected, temporarily but for no reason that a child could understand, from her home into one of strangers. Has trauma like this ever happened to you, or anyone you know?

Mary was not responsible for what had happened to her in her childhood; indeed, she was an innocent victim of circumstance and others' decisions. However, how responsible was she for the actions she took as she—prematurely, by today's standards—moved into adulthood? Was she still a victim of her past? Did early psychological trauma set her up for more? Was she predisposed to make poor decisions? Questions to think about as I tell more of her story.

Shortly after Mary returned to England, a new acolyte of her father's appeared—a young man named Percy Bysshe Shelley who espoused political ideas that were labeled as "seditious" and "blasphemous." He also wrote poetry that, thanks to Mary's later efforts, would cause him to be dubbed "the great Romantic poet." Only five years her senior and very attractive, Percy was married with two children. I am not being glib when I say that one thing led to another between Mary and Percy . . .

At age 17, Mary left her home in England again, this time fleeing with Percy, along with one of her stepsisters as a "companion," a gesture to respectability. Nonetheless, scandal ensued. And nonetheless, onward Mary went to the next stage of her life.

Mary became pregnant by Percy and—after his wife, also pregnant, died by suicide—married him. As was the case with Mary's parents, this move seemed more expedient than sentimental. It was largely aimed at ensuring the legitimacy of their relationship and that of their child, and to secure Percy's hold on his other children. Withal, they continued to be ostracized because so much sensation attached to them.

Whatever one thinks of marriage as an institution, it is based on the desirability of financial and emotional stability, especially when children are involved. Society has come to deem marriage as important. Respectability, too, however that is defined (and the definition can change!). These factors were not necessarily present in the norm-busting time in which Mary Shelley lived. Even so, there seemed to be an inordinate number of people mating and producing children into fluid relationships, of semi-related and illegitimate (terrible word) children living in the same household. Why?

The death of their premature baby was followed by other pregnancies and child-deaths, as well as a miscarriage that nearly took Mary's life. As one of Mary's biographers expressed it,

"The motherless child became a childless mother." (The final child thrived, though; we'll see later that he became a joy to Mary.)

Percy Bysshe Shelley wrote verse about this time in their lives. See if you think his words are more about his loss of her than her loss of her children:

> *My dearest Mary, wherefore hast thou gone,*
> *And left me in this dreary world alone?*
> *Thy form is here indeed—a lovely one—*
> *But thou art fled, gone down a dreary road*
> *That leads to Sorrow's most obscure abode.*
> *For thine own sake I cannot follow thee*
> *Do thou return for mine.*

Throughout their seven years together, which ended in 1822 with Percy's drowning death in Italy, Mary and Percy roamed within England and throughout Italy, Germany, France, and Switzerland.

The two were part of a notorious coterie that included Lord Byron (who, by the way, had impregnated Mary's stepsister) and other Romantic thinkers and writers. Although money was often an issue, they seemed to travel easily from castle to villa to house to yet other villas and castles. Sightseeing and socializing, reading and writing, occupied much time. Always present were assorted spouses, lovers, friends, siblings, cousins, children— legitimate and otherwise. Pregnancies, births, deaths, suicides, and every kind of intrigue and entanglement seemed to characterize the life of this group. As did brilliant creativity.

The genesis of *Frankenstein* is a marvelously illustrative episode. One night in 1816, Lord Byron proposed an amusement to the group—that each person compete to write the "best" horror story. Whatever the prize was, Mary won it. Her story was about Dr. Frankenstein, a scientist who "makes" a creature, a manlike monster of a creature who remains unnamed and who forces his creator to "make" a companion for him. Needless to say, there is no good end for these attempts to replicate God.

I admit that I am being arch in my summary of Mary's book, yet there is much to admire about it. Not least is its longevity: In written form and with various film, TV, comic book, and stage treatments, it has captivated audiences for two hundred plus years. Its themes are profound, centering on human longings and the dangers of over-reaching one's natural place in the scheme of things, of usurping divine powers. Most importantly, though, it showcases a creative process that was both specific to Mary and universal. Mary's talent was unique, but her process is available to any of us.

What do I mean? First of all, she knew her craft. She embraced an inheritance of literacy from her parents, she grew up in a literate environment, she traveled in a literate crowd. And she worked at her craft; we know how prolifically she wrote throughout her life. She took writing seriously as a way to express herself and to make a living, especially after Percy's death.

With this as her foundation, Mary was able to create. She picked and chose among the details of her young life to weave reality, emotion, personal experience, and fantasy together into a seamless tapestry. Longings resulting from the losses she had endured—her experience of the interplay between death and life—her awareness of alchemy, scientific investigations, and experimental techniques such as "galvanism" (which inspired Dr. Frankenstein's application of life-giving electrical impulses into his monster)—her own vivid Romantic-era imagination—all these were influences on her horror story.

When the story was complete, Percy Bysshe Shelley helped edit it and bring it to publication (with an "anonymous" author) on January 1, 1818. It was Mary's first book; she was 21. Because Percy had written (and signed) its introduction, he was initially credited with authorship. That misapprehension was soon rectified, and, after an initially disappointing public reception, *Frankenstein* began to soar.

★ ★ ★

Throughout their lives, the Shelleys had fraught paternal relationships. In Percy's case, this was largely due to his wealthy father's extreme disapproval of his son's dissolute lifestyle, expressed by frequent threats to withdraw or somehow subvert Percy's inheritance. Mary's case was more complicated. Certainly, a factor was her early and quite valid experiences of parental abandonment, regardless of the cause. And she often needed her father's financial help, both during her short marriage and when she became a widow at such a young age. But there was also a great need, at all times, for her father's approval.

William Godwin had definitely not approved when Mary ran off with Percy and they commenced their unusual life together. Perhaps William's attitude changed after the younger man's death. In any event, an example of Mary possibly receiving the approval she craved can be seen in an excerpt from a letter she received from her father after Percy's death. Reminding her that *Frankenstein* was excellent and that she had a solid grasp on her future, Godwin wrote:

> [The book] is the most wonderful work to have been written at twenty years of age that I ever heard of. You are now five and twenty. And, most fortunately, you have pursued a course of reading, and cultivated your mind in a manner the most admirably adapted to make you a great and successful author. If you cannot be independent, who should be?

That last line, though . . . Is that the father telling the daughter not to expect anything from him? At the very least, is it a backhanded compliment? As I said, a fraught relationship.

And there is Mary's second book, a novella written in 1819 after the deaths of two of her children. She sent the manuscript to her father, asking him to publish it. He was reportedly so scandalized that he never responded and refused even to return the manuscript, despite her appeals. That book was unpublished when Mary died, and remained so for a century, until 1959.

Called *Mathilda* (or *Matilda*, no relation to Roald Dahl's character of the same name), it is a paragon of a Gothic horror story. It centers on a tragic young woman on her deathbed, narrating her life's story to a male friend, a gifted poet. It involves fantasy. It is peopled by an idealized deceased mother and a depressed father who commits suicide after attempting incest with the narrator. Was Mary's book a plea for approval that went unanswered? A desperate cry of some kind? What are we to make of details that seem autobiographical but may not be? Regardless of (because of?) these unanswered (unanswerable?) questions, many consider *Matilda* to be on par with *Frankenstein* in Mary's body of work.

Earlier, I mentioned that Mary's surviving child was a source of great joy to her. Named Percy Florence (because of his birthplace) Shelley, he was by all accounts devoted to his mother; he married a woman equally devoted to Mary. Upon inheriting his paternal grandfather's baronetcy in 1844, he was given the honorific "Sir" and the title of the 3rd Baronet of Castle Goring. He was a minor politician, an amateur actor, a yachtsman, and a "gentleman."

Before her death in 1851, Mary had requested that she be buried with her parents; Mary Wollstonecraft had died in 1797, as we know, and William in 1836. Their cemetery, St. Pancras in London, had been where William taught his little daughter to read her mother's gravestone. But St. Pancras had fallen into such ruin, that Sir Percy re-interpreted his mother's request. He exhumed his grandparents' remains and moved them to the Shelley family vault at St. Peter's Church in Bournemouth. With Mary reposing there as well, perhaps her attachment issues were put to rest. The graves of Sir Percy and his wife are also in the family vault.

A final detail befitting these people of the Romantic Era:

When Percy Bysshe Shelley drowned so many years earlier and his body had washed ashore, the Italian authorities had insisted that he be cremated on the beach where he lay. Supposedly Mary was able to secure his heart. Supposedly, it was found, wrapped in a cloth and kept among her possessions, after her death. And supposedly, this heart was buried alongside Sir Percy, so all could be together for all time.

3

HONORÉ DAUMIER
(France)

THE TURNING POINT IN THE PROFESSIONAL LIFE of the
nineteenth-century artist Honoré Daumier came when he was
22 years old, at one of the many turning points in the national life of the French.

Daumier was about five years into his nascent career as a
commercial lithographer, making plates for publishers of sheet
music and advertisements. He had lofty dreams of an artistic
life, and was cultivating his own style of realistic drawing, but
right then he needed to make a living. Putting the work of others out into the world would have to do for now.

In late July of 1830, his country was roiled by yet another
upheaval, the Second French Revolution (also called the July
Revolution). Turmoil in the conservative government of the
deeply unpopular King Charles X had culminated in the impo-
sition of the "July Ordinances." Among other "reforms," the
Ordinances re-instated Napoleon-era press censorship. Within
a week, riots broke out and in a three-day-long rebellion—*Les
Trois Glorieuses*—Charles was dethroned. His replacement was
the more liberal and popular (for a time) Louis-Philippe I.

The time was right for Honoré Daumier.

I can empathize with his situation; can you? Maybe he was
bored at the print shop, too young to be tied down with a predictable future ahead of him. Maybe he was actively looking for

new opportunity; not everyone looks for it, recognizes it, or is brave enough to grasp it, because opportunity can be risky. Maybe his social conscience had been pricked by what he had already seen of injustice and disadvantage in his life, and he was stirred by his own rebellion.

And maybe Daumier was canny enough to see the import of an emerging market: weekly magazines, newspapers, and journals that, in those pre-photography days, relied on graphic illustrations—lithographs—to accompany their stories. Just as there was plenty to write about in a society filled with controversy, there was plenty to draw about.

For Daumier, the apparent recommitment of the government to freedom of the press—combined with more ways to exercise this freedom—was exciting. He decided to turn his life in a different direction, at age 22. He joined the staff of *La Caricature*, a new journal devoted to written and visual political satire, as a cartoonist. It's safe to say that he would never be bored in his work again.

Still using the medium of lithography, Daumier put his drawing and printmaking skills to use in a more imaginative way. Now he could express his own viewpoints. He became an artist who changed the way people looked at the world. His concerns about power and justice were specific to his time, and based on his personal experiences and observations, yet they remain perennial. Indeed, it has been said of his works, "their graphic power carries them beyond their period and its politics."

Lithography is a printing process that uses a flat stone or metal plate on which the image areas are worked (drawn) using a greasy substance so that the ink will adhere to them, while the non-image areas are made ink-repellent. Its invention (in the late eighteenth century) made it possible to print a much wider range of marks and areas of tone than possible with earlier printmaking methods. It also made color printing easier: Areas of different colors can be applied to separate stones and overprinted onto the same sheet. *(Tate Museum, UK)*

Throughout his nearly fifty-year career, Daumier would skewer the powerful of France in some four thousand lithographs, and in wood engravings, drawings, and sculptures numbering another two thousand or so. No one in the monarchy, the Church or the bourgeoisie—no one in society or politics—was safe from his scrutiny. At the same time, much of his work cast a sympathetic eye on "regular" and poor people whose lives had only gotten worse from the effects of, for example, industrialization.

There was another aspect to Daumier's long career. He eventually developed into a prolific portrait, landscape, and genre painter. He produced around five hundred oils and watercolors that garnered little or no attention from the public during his lifetime, to his disappointment. Posthumously, though, critics saw in this work a foretaste of impressionism, the art movement that had just appeared on the horizon, and appreciation rose.

My interest in Daumier was piqued by my late colleague John Kasic, who had studied the artist for many years and who had helped create a collection of Daumier prints, paintings, and books for my home.

Honoré Daumier was born on February 26, 1808, in Marseille, in the south of France. He was the only child of his parents. His father was a second-generation glazier and framemaker. When Honoré was 7 or 8 years old, the father left his business, uprooted his wife and his son, and headed north. It seems that the older man was also "an eccentric . . . with high-flown poetic ambitions *(who)* took his family to Paris in pursuit of his doomed literary projects," according to the National Gallery of Art in Washington, D.C.

With his father having abandoned his business and having never really recovered from being "doomed" in his ambitions, young Honoré had to go to work at age 12 or 13 to help support the family. He became a messenger for a bailiff, an experience that probably helped form the jaundiced view of the law courts that is so sharply reflected in his later works. He then worked as a bookseller's clerk at the Palais-Royal, one of the social hubs of Paris then as now, a place where he could observe the passing parade of dandies, overdressed ladies, bankers, businessmen, politicians, and hangers-on who would later become the subjects of his searing caricatures.

Although Honoré showed an early talent for drawing, his parents either could not afford to send him for formal instruction or—perhaps because of the father's mental breakdown over his failure as a poet—wanted to steer him in a more practical direction. Undeterred, Honoré took informal drawing lessons from a family friend, drew from life at a teacher-less and inexpensive art school, and copied sculptures and portraits onto his sketch pad at the Louvre. Time-honored methods of artistic self-education.

A museum official who was apparently impressed by his talent convinced Daumier's parents that they should let him become an artist. And so, at age 17 while holding a job in a commercial print shop making plates for customers, Honoré began developing his distinctive style of realistic drawing that formed the foundation of both his graphic and his painterly work.

And then came the events of July 1830, the platform presented by the visibility of La Caricature and the realization that what he could say and show through his own art might matter.

Daumier found much to satirize in the new government. Although Louis-Philippe avoided many of the personal excesses of his ousted predecessor, his political support came from the wealthy class, whose standing only rose while conditions among the working poor and the unemployed deteriorated.

A caricature is a painting, or more usually drawing, of a person or thing in which the features and form have been distorted and exaggerated in order to mock or satirize the subject. *(Tate Museum, UK)*

Remember the freedom of the press that Louis-Philippe's ascension to the throne supposedly heralded? It was short-lived. Daumier's satire proved to be too much, especially when he lampooned the new king with a lithograph called "Gargantua" that depicted the bloated monarch seated on his throne consuming bags of coins being dragged into his presence by downtrodden workers. Police halted the printing of the issue of *La Caricature* in which "Gargantua" appeared before it could complete its run, and Daumier was fined and sentenced to six months in prison.

The year was 1832, and at age 24 Daumier had made the first of his many marks. He went on to become a master of caricature, among the most well-known of the many practitioners in France in a golden age for that art form in England and the United States as well. His reputation remains intact now over 140 years after his death. He was active in so many artistic media that, as the Getty Museum says, his creations "comprise the largest visual legacy of any artist before 1900."

I find much to admire in Honoré Daumier in his early career. Clearly, he was ambitious; he was also brave. He was devoted to his craft and flexible in his approach to new situations. And he certainly knew how to communicate, a judgment I can make based on my years in the business of public relations.

After "Gargantua" and the 1832 imprisonment, a lesser person might have been daunted. Instead, Daumier continued with his politically charged artwork for *La Caricature*. He even went on to make satirical clay figurines of members of the French parliament, the National Assembly, along with lithographic caricatures that were collected in a work called "Le Ventre legislative," which translates roughly as "The Legislative Belly."

La Caricature folded in 1835, a victim of the tightening government noose on press freedom. Not so different from today. We see many examples of repression and suppression aimed at satire, which often has the effect of causing more repression and suppression. The process circles viciously.

> The terms "political satire" and "social satire" are very closely linked, sometimes being used interchangeably. They both are ways to expose and criticize the behavior of others via humor, exaggeration, ridicule, etc. Political satire, because it is most often aimed at prominent people holding actual governmental power, attracts repression, suppression, and censorship much more readily than does satire aimed at socialites and their foibles. A magazine satirizing the folks at a dinner party or a gala might—*might*—invite a lawsuit, but not a police-enforced shutdown.

Daumier, age 27, moved to the publisher's other journal, *Le Charivari* ("pandemonium"), which focused on more broadly based and acceptable social satire, rather than on the political. And so now he turned his sharp eye on Parisian society, from fussy bourgeoisie, to pompous aristocrats, to arrogant lawyers, to callous bankers, to rapacious landlords—and just about everyone in between.

As Daumier matured, he became more exploratory in his use of medium (he taught himself watercolor and oil painting techniques and expanded his sculpturing) and in his subject matter ("popular" and non-controversial landscapes, for example). He seemed to be making art more for his own satisfaction, I think, rather than as public statements. As much as I admire his early career, I also admire his ability, in his later years, to turn inward and to cultivate a spirit of constant renewal. Valuable lessons for any age.

At the same time, the upheavals and calamities of his era continued unabated. Louis-Philippe and his so-called July Monarchy—indeed, the entire French system of monarchy—gave way in 1848 to a conservative elected republic, which fell in the 1851 coup d'état that installed an autocratic president. And on and on. Each development offered obvious targets for Daumier's rapier-like graphic work and his withering caricatures. That continued until government censorship once again forced Daumier to return to relatively harmless social caricatures for *Le Charivari*.

After 1853 (age 45), he began a circular process of retiring to work on his own, and then returning to the public eye and then retiring again. Reluctant to leave the field of battle behind him, it seems, when there was still so much to say and do. He was fired from *Le Charivari* in 1860 and then invited back four years later. He finally left Paris for a small house in the country, where he lived quietly with his wife (their child had died in 1848 at age 2) and declined the offer of a government award.

His eyesight began to fail and the visual details that anchored his work became more difficult to achieve. Even so, the Franco-Prussian War of 1870–1871 was artistically and thematically energizing. According to the National Gallery, "Some of Daumier's most powerful lithographs date from this time," as the tragedies of war followed by civil strife inflicted terrible suffering on working people and the poor.

Blind and impoverished, Daumier died at age 71 on February 10, 1879. He left behind a great number of unfinished paintings, which must have been a sorrow to him, but because of his lithography, his place in the canon of political art was already assured and only grows more secure.

★ ★ ★

Writing about Honoré Daumier, I kept thinking about the terrorist attack that took place in 2015 at the offices of *Charlie Hebdo*, a prominent and long-standing satirical newsweekly based in Paris. The mass shooting, which left twelve employees dead and eleven others wounded, was retaliation for the publication of caricatures deemed offensive to a group of extremists. Honoré Daumier would have found fertile ground for his work at *Charlie Hebdo*, I think. He would have recognized the need for free expression that the newspaper represented, as well as the anger such expression can provoke.

Every era in history has needed artists, writers, comedians, graphic designers, commentators, pundits, and others to pull the curtain aside, à la Dorothy's dog Toto in *The Wizard of Oz*, and show us what's really going on. Every era has had such people, and Daumier occupies a notable place in the long line of political and social satirists.

Political satire, specifically, gets tangled up in issues of authoritarianism and censorship and liability and invasions of privacy and freedom of the press (freedom of *all* media, now; we're way beyond the illustrated journals of Daumier's time). Danger can be the result. In a never-ending cycle, satire can cause crackdowns by actual or self-proclaimed "authorities," governmental or other; crackdowns inspire more satire and then more crackdowns. Add in extremist groups who despise satire, and the result can be a *Charlie Hebdo* event.

Prison and a fine did not stop Honoré Daumier from following his calling. What happened to him in Paris in the 1830s is trivial compared with what happened in Paris in 2015. But the terrorist attacks did not stop *Charlie Hebdo* and its people either. The newsweekly continued publishing on schedule, as it had done since its founding in 1970 (though with a hiatus from 1981 to 1992, when it was relaunched).

4

ULYSSES S. GRANT
(United States)

THE MORAL OF THIS STORY IS THAT it takes some people a long time to get where they are going. And there can be many detours along the way.

Was Ulysses S. Grant one of the five greatest generals in U.S. history? Was he one of the ten worst presidents in U.S. history? Was he just a drunk?

For too many of us, Ulysses S. Grant, commander of the Union Army from 1863 to 1865 and president of the United States from 1869 to 1877, exists as an outline of a figure, a silhouette, with no real content. Yes, his troops defeated the Confederacy and saved the United States. Yes, his administration was rife with corruption and controversy, especially in his second term, even as it advanced causes of social justice. And yes, he was almost certainly an alcoholic, in today's understanding of that condition as a disease and not a sign of moral weakness. And that's about all we know, or care to know.

But if we look closely, as I have done—because people whose opinion I value suggested that he be included in this book— Grant emerges as a surprisingly compelling and sympathetic figure. He came from nothing, was on the verge of making something of himself at age 26, and lost his way by age 32. It took him almost a decade to regain his footing. His accomplishments came in middle age—he was 41 when Lincoln gave him his life-changing assignment, 47 when he was elected president. And then, he stumbled again. How human!

Grant seemed to have no illusions about himself, a refreshing quality. In the preface to his memoirs, which he wrote in 1885 when he was on the verge of death, he said, "There are but few important events in the affairs of men brought about by their own choice."

Until 1848, at age 26, Grant could claim little that was his "own choice"; rather, he had mostly accepted what those in authority wanted him to do. He had gone to West Point only because his father wanted him to. When he graduated from the famed military academy in 1843, he was unhappy about his infantry assignment, but of course he had to accept it. His humble ambition was to teach mathematics at a university, perhaps even at West Point, but that would have to wait until the army gave its approval. Because he was a soldier, trained for war, when war came (Mexican American, 1846–1848), he followed orders and waged it; quite honorably so.

Grant wasn't following orders but making his "own choice" when he proposed marriage to Julia Dent, the sister of a West Point classmate. They wed in 1848 and would have four children, all of whom lived into adulthood, a true accomplishment in those days. The "family circle" was known for its happiness and mutual devotion.

That war was a turning point. Grant had been utterly ordinary for most of his life. A nice enough guy, whose friends and family loved him. No one really expected much of him. In fact, most of us *are* ordinary. We often come face-to-face with that reality at the cusp of our adult lives—defined, in this book, as around age 25 or so—which can be a disheartening and tough time of wondering "what it's all about."

> If we are fortunate, there are people at all times in our lives who think we are special, in addition to being ordinary: parents, friends, spouses, partners, teachers, colleagues, mentors, children, patrons. They help us become who we are meant to be.

At his own cusp, because of his war service, Grant came face-to-face with himself and decided that he was no longer ordinary. He had always been a reluctant warrior, but now he began to trust in his abilities as a soldier. A mathematics professor he was not to be. Instead, winning promotion to the rank of first lieutenant, he made the choice at age 26 to embrace his future as a fighting man. Within six years, that future would lie in tatters, by his own hand. In 1854, he resigned from the army, if not in disgrace, certainly under a cloud. He was 32 and needed to start over. Seven years later, as the Civil War began, he would be back in the army.

Most of us have had to start over again, for one reason or another. I certainly have, and I remember those times as very unsettling. When I look back, I can see that it all made sense, but it didn't seem that way when I was in the midst of great uncertainty.

Let's take a look at Ulysses Grant's early life, as a way to appreciate how easily he might *not* have regrouped from his career disaster in 1854. His future as an acclaimed general and an initially popular, though eventually problematic, president was by no means assured.

Hiram Ulysses Grant was born on April 27, 1822, in Point Pleasant, Ohio, the first child of his parents Jesse and Hannah.

"Hiram" was his maternal grandfather's name and "Ulysses" was randomly chosen; the child would always be called "Ulysses." The next year, the family moved some miles away to Georgetown, where five more children were born, and enjoyed "comfortable circumstances."

Eight generations earlier, in 1630, Ulysses's forbears on his father's side arrived at the Massachusetts Bay Colony; this explains the quiet pride with which he opened chapter one of his memoirs: "My family is American, and has been for generations, in all its branches, direct and collateral." Grant men were soldiers, serving and sometimes dying, in the French and Indian War (1754–1763) and in the American Revolution, specifically at the Battle of Bunker Hill (1775). Over the years, the family had made its way from New England through Pennsylvania into Ohio, where in 1820 Jesse found work as a tanner and married Hannah in 1821. Ohio was considered "the West" then, and Ulysses would enfold his origins there into his identity.

As young Ulysses grew up, he was an obedient and amiable fellow, almost always doing just what he was told to do without much fuss.

I'll quote liberally from Grant's memoirs two chapters on his childhood, adolescence and his time at West Point. These are relatively short chapters in a very long book (seventy chapters), probably because, as he wrote of his youth, "my life was uneventful."

I find the early chapters of Grant's two-volume memoir invaluable because they communicate the peace, stability, and regularity—the ordinariness—that underpinned his early life. They're also interesting! And some of his language may be archaic, but it's charming. His entire, minutely detailed memoir, "dedicated to the American soldier and sailor," is as subjective as anyone else's would be. It tells us what he wanted us to know, nothing more and nothing less.

Schooling and work were Ulysses's primary occupations, because both were important to his father, a man who was not well-educated but knew the value of education and who, as a self-made man, knew the value of his own labor.

Because Jesse was "mindful of his own lack of facilities for acquitting an education, his greatest desire in maturer (sic) years was for the education of his children." Consequently, from the age of 5 or 6, until he left Georgetown for West Point at age 17, Ulysses "never missed a quarter from school."

Schools in that time and place were "very indifferent." They were run mostly by "subscription" (similar to tuition, with money paid directly to the teacher, who may or may not have had any training or other qualifications); students could also live away at "private" schools and pay room and board in addition to tuition. Ulysses attended both types. He wrote many years later of his time away at private school: "I was not studious in habit, and probably did not make progress enough to compensate for the outlay of board and tuition."

Schooling, indifferent or not, "did not exempt me from labor," wrote Grant. And that was most definitely true. His father was involved in both the manufacture of leather and farmed the considerable land he owned. Ulysses hated the leather trade, but was, as he wrote, "fond of agriculture, and of all employment in which horses could be used."

Ulysses "detested" the tannery because of the blood, gore, and terrible smells associated with processing animal skins into leather. His father might have been insulted by his son's reaction to the work that put food on the family table, but the fact that Ulysses worked so hard at everything else mitigated any criticism. He didn't like to work, he admitted in self-deprecation, "but I did as much of it, while young, as grown men can be hired to do in these days and attended school at the same time."

Even at age 7 and 8, he was hauling wood cut from the family's fifty acres of forest; at age 11, though it sounds like exhausting child labor to us, he was doing what was expected and what was helpful to his family—plowing the fields, planting corn and potatoes, harvesting crops, and sawing up the wood that he had hauled in into pieces that would fit in the stove. All this while still going to school.

What Ulysses really loved was working with horses. He and the animals seemed to understand each other instinctively and, even when he was a very small child, he played safely under and around them. In addition, they tapped an entrepreneurial streak: As a teenager, he ran a business of driving people throughout Ohio and into Kentucky and Virginia, wherever they might need to go.

As important as school and work were to Jesse, the man was not a stern taskmaster for his eldest son. In fact, both parents indulged him and his tractable personality but did not spoil him. Ulysses thus seemed to lead an almost idyllic boy's life in Georgetown. As he himself wrote, "I had as many privileges as any boy in the village, and probably more than most of them. I have no recollection of ever having been punished at home, either by scolding or the rod."

Biographers have focused on Ulysses's relationship with his father in ways that, understandably, did not appear in his memoirs. To use a colloquialism, Jesse "bragged on" his son—he exaggerated the import of anything that Ulysses did, even the most ordinary and non-consequential. Ulysses never bragged on himself, but sometimes people in the community made fun of him anyway.

Who knows where 17-year-old Ulysses thought his future lay? He did want to continue to travel, because he prided himself that he "was already the best traveled boy in Georgetown," having gone as far away as fifty miles from home. But he really had no idea of what might be ahead of him.

His father did, though, and at the Christmas holidays of 1838–1839, he unveiled his plan to the oblivious Ulysses. Here is the story as told in Grant's memoir, a story included in so many of his biographers' books:

During this vacation my father received a letter from the Honorable Thomas Morris, then United Sates Senator from Ohio. When he read it, he said to me, "Ulysses, I believe you are going to receive the appointment." "What appointment?" I inquired. "To West Point; I have applied for it." "But I won't go," I said. He said he thought I would, *and I thought so too, if he did* [emphasis as it appears in Grant's book].

I'll pause here and ask two simple questions: Have you ever been on either side of a conversation like that? How did it go?

Putting aside the fact that Ulysses had no choice in the matter, what troubled him about West Point was that he "could not bear the idea of failing." I certainly understand that trepidation. Self-deluded, he was not.

Regardless, off he went obediently, leaving Georgetown for New York—all alone, first by river steamer, then on canal "packets" and finally by rail—in mid-May 1839. The fact that he traveled by packet on the second leg of his trip was telling; he could have taken a stagecoach, but it would have been faster, and he was in no hurry to reach his destination.

He arrived at West Point at the end of May, took and passed his entrance exams without much difficulty, then settled into a military life that "had no charms for me." He decided then and there that even if he graduated, which he did not expect to do, he would not stay in the army. He did, however, recognize that "if a man graduates here, he is safe for life," no matter where he went afterward.

Is it possible that his ambivalence was due to being homesick? He was young and presumably immature, away from home for the first time, in what may as well have been a foreign country (he was a Westerner, and many things were different in New York). How well I remember that feeling in college; I have also observed the effects when others feel alienated, when they are trying to settle into new places and situations.

Ulysses arrived at West Point amid a bit of confusion about his name. He never used his given name "Hiram," so he enrolled as Ulysses Grant. Somehow, he ended up with a middle initial (perhaps after his mother's maiden name of Simpson, but in reality, the "S" didn't stand for anything). Unlike Harry S Truman, who also acquired a middle initial, Ulysses always punctuated his "S": he was "Ulysses S. Grant." He was sometimes teased as "Uncle Sam" at West Point, for obvious reasons.

Eventually he wrote in a letter to a cousin: "There is much to dislike but more to like. On the whole, I like the place very much, so much that I would not go away on any account." Eventually he scraped his way through West Point, and in 1843 he graduated twenty-first in a class of thirty-nine, never having held any position of cadet leadership.

But there were strengths that became evident during his years at West Point. First, despite his meager background in Georgetown's "indifferent" schools, Ulysses found that he was very good at mathematics. He dreamed—it was not quite an ambition and would remain an unfulfilled dream—that he could get a post as an assistant professor of mathematics at the academy and go on to a permanent position as professor at a good college.

Second, it became evident that he was a horseman with few peers. His true gift, for that's what it was, had emerged at home in Ohio but blossomed at West Point where his horsemanship was legendary. Perhaps out of modesty, Grant does not detail this, but his biographers did. One, H. W. Brands, wrote that he made a deep impression on his classmates by jumping his horse over a six-foot-high barrier.

After graduation, unfortunately, the cavalry where he expected to be assigned was closed off to him, probably because the U.S. Army had only one such regiment, and that, plus his undistinguished class standing, was a handicap. There were, however, plenty of infantry assignments; he was given one, and in September 1843, at age 21, he took his first posting, at Jefferson Barracks, Missouri.

Is it enough to say *que serà, serà,* or *c'est la vie,* or "those are the breaks"? To suck it up, grow a spine . . . and move forward, regardless? Ulysses Grant must have thought so. Onward he dutifully went to Missouri; he had to.

The light in his life during his first posting was meeting and falling in love with Julia Dent in 1844; two years later came the two-year Mexican American War. His correspondence with Julia during those war years did not stint on details of the horrors of firsthand combat he experienced throughout Mexico. He also was candid about his continuing ambivalence regarding his career. From a letter: "In the course of a few months more I will see you again if it costs my commission, which by the way I value very low."

And yet Grant performed bravely during the war and was among those who marched victorious into Mexico City in late 1847. The peace treaty was signed in May 1848 and Grant was on his way, as quickly as allowed, home to marry Julia and enjoy a short leave before taking his next posting. As I wrote earlier in the chapter, his war service had confirmed his resolve as a soldier.

Even infantrymen such as Grant rode horses. Consider this episode of his brave horsemanship, when he volunteered for a dangerous assignment during a battle in the Mexican village of Monterey. According to his memoirs: "My ride back was an exposed one. Before starting I adjusted myself on the side of my horse furthest from the enemy, and with only one foot holding to the cantle of the saddle, and an arm over the neck

> of the horse exposed, I started at full run. It was only at
> street crossings that my horse was under fire, but these I
> crossed at such a flying rate that generally I was past and
> under cover of the next block of houses before the enemy
> fired. I got out safely without a scratch."

In 1852, the Fourth Regiment, to which Grant was assigned, was sent on a new mission, protecting the West Coast,
which the United States had acquired as a result of the war with
Mexico. Grant had to depart from Julia, pregnant with their
second child, and their 2-year-old son. A challenging deploy-
ment in Oregon and Northern California followed. The military assignment was both difficult and boring; yellow fever was
rampant; Grant missed his family dearly and often worried that
Julia had forgotten him. He probably also suffered from what
we now call seasonal affective disorder (sunlight is a challenge
on the Pacific Northwest coast most months of the year). Grant
began to drink. Many other soldiers, many other people, have
done the same in an effort to cope.

And now to the elephant in the room. Grant would be
known as a drinker for the rest of his life, perhaps unfairly so,
perhaps accurately. His memoirs say nothing about any drinking, ever. Some of his biographers overlook the rumors completely or mention them only in passing; others do not mince
words about the drinking culture that flourished in Grant's regiment. Ron Chernow, in his 2017 book *Grant*, was most
forthright in his assessment that Grant was a true alcoholic. The
fact appears to be that Grant could go for months without any
liquor, then suffer a temporarily debilitating binge, and then re-
sume his responsibilities seemingly without missing a beat. He
was dependent on alcohol to function, but he *did* function very
well, better than many.

What are we to make of this? As I ponder Grant's story, I

come away accepting the truth that we never know everything about someone else, nor do we necessarily have the right to such knowledge. What I believe is that, whether from cause or correlation, his drinking temporarily cost him his army career. We do know that after one very embarrassing episode, he resigned his commission in April 1854.

Unemployed, Grant fearfully returned to Julia, who was living at her parents' home in Missouri with their two children (the second of which he had yet to meet). Though he remained unemployed, he need not have feared his wife. "How happy this reunion was!" she wrote later. More difficult was the humiliating trip to Ohio to face directly the opprobrium of his father who did not hide his disapproval of Grant's resignation or of his state of unemployment.

How miserable he must have been. Whatever self-knowledge he had acquired six years earlier in the wake of the Mexican American War and just before his marriage to Julia seemed to disappear. Apparently, he *was* ordinary, perhaps worse than ordinary. At age 32, he started over, beginning a slog through civilian life. Two more children were born. Try as he might, success as a farmer and a hardware store proprietor eluded him. And the Civil War was inexorably bearing down on the country.

In 1861, at age 39, his dormant soldier's instinct must have kicked in. He heeded the call for volunteer troops to defend the Union and was able to rejoin the army. He rose to the occasion. He was so effective that two years later Lincoln chose him as the Commanding General of the Union Army. As we all know that army was victorious; in 1865, the Civil War was over, and Grant's acclaim knew no bounds.

Recall the words I quoted earlier from the preface of Grant's memoirs: "There are but few important events in the affairs of men brought about by their own choice." Note that Lincoln *chose* him. Note that in 1868 the Republican Party *chose* him to run for president. Note that the American people *chose* him as president later that year and again four years later. But note also, that it was *Grant*'s choice to volunteer in 1861 that put him on his path to accomplishment.

Grant acceded to the will of others one more time. Destitute and facing death in 1885, and worried about how to provide for Julia, he accepted a publisher's offer for his memoirs; twenty years after the Civil War, the public's interest in his exploits was as intense as ever.

Sometimes long-standing but underdeveloped strengths come back to us in later life. We remember what we used to be good at, or what we used to enjoy. As cancer ravaged him, Grant seemed to reach back almost forty-five years to his time at West Point, when he had discovered that he was "a writer of confident, limber English prose." It was a talent that he sharpened during a lifetime of letter writing and brought to a high point during the war when, according to Bunting's biography, "No commander wrote more lucid, more accurate, or more orderly communications."

As he set about writing his memoirs, Grant made a few false starts. When his publisher counseled him to write "conversationally," as if he were telling a story to a companion, it all began flowing smoothly, and he actually enjoyed the process. He worked up to six hours a day, or as much as his dwindling strength and great pain would allow; an assistant helped him with fact-checking. He took his story up until the end of the Civil War, choosing not to treat his presidency or postpresidency.

Satisfied with his work, on July 16 he laid down the soft pencil he liked to write with. He died exactly a week later, at age 63, on July 23, 1885.

To sell the book, a marketing campaign ensued that would be the envy of any author today. Clever salesmanship, and the quality of Grant's work, assured that 300,000 copies of *Personal Memoirs* were sold within two years; $450,000 in royalties soon accrued to Julia Grant.

Proof that the book continues to have resonance and relevance is that it has never been out of print. Perhaps this is why: The final chapter contains words we should all take to heart, Grant's hopes for the future of America:

> We have but little to do [except] to preserve peace, happiness and prosperity at home, and the respect of other nations. Our experience ought to teach us the necessity of the first; our power secures the latter.

5

ALBERT EINSTEIN
(Germany, United States)

To many, it's obvious why Albert Einstein is in this book. Wasn't Einstein that poor misunderstood guy who spent most of his twenties moldering six days a week at a clerk's desk in an office, mindlessly processing patent applications from people who couldn't hold a candle to his genius? We know now what he would become, but who knew then, in the first decade of the twentieth century?

"How ironic!" it's tempting to say. Or "There's hope for all of us. Maybe he was just a late bloomer." Or "What a waste of his potential!"

I propose an alternate scenario—that the seven years that Einstein spent as a junior employee at the Federal Office for Intellectual Property in Berne, Switzerland, were an intensely creative period for him, a time of incubation for the discoveries in physics that would make him the greatest scientist of the twentieth century.

It was in the middle of those years, in 1905, that Einstein completed his PhD thesis and published four foundational papers that presented discoveries on a par with those of Galileo and Newton. His fourth paper contained his "special theory of relativity" and the most famous equation in the world: $E = mc^2$. Ten years later, his "general theory of relativity" would emerge and in 1921, he would win the Nobel Prize in Physics.

What is physics? "The branch of science concerned with the nature and properties of matter and energy. The subject matter of physics, distinguished from that of chemistry and biology, includes mechanics, heat, light and other radiation, sound, electricity, magnetism and the structure of atoms."
—*Oxford Dictionary*

The year 1905 would come to be called Einstein's *annus mirabilis*—his "amazing year"—but at the time, this was the reality:

Einstein was a 26-year-old high school dropout and a draft dodger who had tried to get into college but failed on his first try, and who had spent much of his time in college dreaming and reading in cafés instead of going to class, so that no professors would give him a recommendation for a job when he graduated, and patent clerk was the only occupation he could find to support himself and his wife and child. Not exactly the moves of a "genius," a word that has become synonymous with his name. Nothing there that presages any accomplishment.

But as dismal as Einstein's situation seems in that telling, consider that for someone who liked to conduct "thought experiments" in his mind, having a boring job that paid the bills might have been just the thing. Many artists and writers and actors—people who work at something or another during the day, then hone their art or their craft in their off-hours, preparing for their big break—would completely understand Einstein's situation.

There is so much that I find compelling in the early life of Einstein, in his first three decades. I will not even scratch the surface of his later years in this chapter; as another genius in another field once said, "You can look it up." I hope that the insights I will share are pertinent to anyone struggling to navigate our very challenging times. And pertinent to anyone trying to encourage others in the struggle.

And for anyone who scoffs and says, "Well, he was *Einstein*, what can he possibly have to do with me? I'm no genius," I offer his own words: "I have no special talents, I am only passionately curious."

Isn't being "passionately curious" within the reach of any of us?

David Bodanis wrote in his 2016 biography *Einstein's Greatest Mistake* that Einstein was "a fallible genius," whose greatest mistake was his stubbornness. Indeed, Einstein was a complex, contradictory, and often difficult man. At the same time, he was a great and brilliant man who sought to understand the great mysteries of time, light, energy, matter, and more. He has much beyond physics to teach us. He overcame adversity (sometimes of his own making), held fast to his own beliefs, challenged himself as much as he challenged others, envisioned a better life, eschewed conventionality, and succeeded mostly on his own terms.

Albert Einstein was born in Ulm, Württemberg, Germany, on March 14, 1879, the first child of his parents Hermann and Pauline, non-observant Ashkenazi Jews. Ulm was a noted center for mathematicians, but Hermann was not inclined toward the sciences; instead, he was a partner in a company that made featherbeds. Pauline came from a wealthy family whose financial support was often necessary to the new family and in later years. Albert's sister Maria (called Maja), with whom he was close their entire lives, was born two years later.

The year after Albert's birth, the family moved to Munich. Featherbedding in Ulm had failed, so Hermann joined his brother in founding an electrical equipment company. In 1894, that company failed, too, largely because its products were based on the prevailing direct-current protocol and it had difficulty adapting to the new alternating current standard. But there were also whiffs of anti-Semitism, as contracts were withdrawn and then awarded to non-Jewish supply houses. At that point, Hermann, Pauline, and Maja moved to Italy, so that Hermann could open yet another business, again with his in-laws' financial support. The 15-year-old Albert was left behind in Munich to finish high school.

Before exploring what being left behind meant for the teenager (abandonment? freedom?), let's take a look at Albert's childhood and early teen years in Munich.

In many ways, his childhood seemed almost enviable. The family was a warm, even gentle one and Albert was given a secure foundation in life as well as love and freedom. His parents *cared* for him, in all senses of that word. Not all of us possess, or have been able to provide to others, that kind of foundation.

Albert's parents had very different personalities that complemented each other rather than conflicted. The happy spouses were loving and devoted parents, and many of Albert's traits and interests throughout his entire life can be traced to their influence. An example is the gift of a compass that his father gave Albert when he was 4 or 5 years old. The fact that the needle seemed controlled by a hidden force fascinated him. Years later he wrote: "This experience made a deep and lasting impression on me . . . Something deeply hidden had to be behind things."

Another example is the gift of violin lessons, beginning around that same age, from his mother, who was herself an accomplished pianist. Albert resented the lessons until he encountered Mozart's sonatas and began playing them with his mother accompanying him on the piano. Experiencing something so moving and beautiful was not only eye-opening for him, he came to believe that it helped him think.

It was when Albert began school at age 6 that his Jewish identity became obvious to the outside world. As I said, his parents were non-observant at home, and thought nothing of sending him to the nearby Catholic school. There he was the only Jew in a large class of children and "did so well in his

Catholic studies that he helped his classmates with theirs," according to one account. But these same classmates also attacked him physically and verbally for being Jewish. A lifelong inner push-pull seemed to develop in Einstein about Judaism in particular and religion in general, very much linked to his explorations of the workings of creation.

Apart from the classroom, the schoolboy Albert opened up in many ways. His uncle taught him algebra, and it became evident that Albert could think "in pictures," turning abstract concepts into something concrete that his mind could manipulate. A medical student who became a family friend taught him geometry from a textbook that Albert fell in love with, calling it his "sacred little geometry book." This same family friend gave him a popular series of illustrated science books for young people, further stimulating Albert to reach beyond what he could see to what he could imagine. I hope you have been both the recipient and the donor of such experiences.

When he was 9 years old, Albert entered "high school"—the Luitpold Gymnasium, which focused on science and mathematics in addition to the classics. This began a problematical time for Albert; like many an accomplished person, he had a series of less-than-ideal educational experiences.

He chafed at the regimentation, rote learning, mindless discipline, and conformity that he was subjected to at school. He was singled out by a teacher who announced to the world that his insolence made him "unwelcome in class." He became very uncomfortable with the glorification of anything military in nature, even otherwise harmless holiday parades when merry students marched in lockstep with soldiers. Eschewing Jewish rituals, he refused a bar mitzvah. He became increasingly resistant to any kind of authority, religious or secular, and to received wisdom whatever its source. These experiences and reactions are not unusual; in Einstein's case, they indicated the independence of thought that would characterize his scientific career.

And then there was the last straw when his family decamped

for Italy (to Pavia, near Milan) in 1894 and expected him to stay in Munich by himself (well, boarding with a distant relative) to finish high school. I'm being gently sarcastic here, but evidence of Einstein's genius—or at least his cleverness—may lie in how he managed to escape his miserable situation and rejoin his family in Milan. He did that, whether intentionally or not, by leaving the Luitpold Gymnasium in the autumn of 1894, either because he was invited to depart or because he was forced out. He then obtained a letter from his family doctor diagnosing him as suffering from nervous exhaustion. That justified his not returning to the school after the Christmas vacation.

Another factor, given his distaste of anything militaristic, was Albert's growing realization that he would be, at age 17, subject to German draft. Not only did leaving Munich remove him from that possibility, he also asked his father's help in renouncing his German citizenship. He would be stateless for five years, becoming a Swiss citizen in 1901 and an American citizen in 1940.

Once he was in Italy, Albert was able to relax and regain his footing. He spent a year working with his uncle and his father, hiking in the mountains, and traveling about. Rather than reentering any secondary school, he began an independent course of study aimed at gaining admission to the Swiss Federal Institute of Technology (now known as ETH Zurich). At age 16, he was too young, but he wangled an exception to take the entrance exams. Albert excelled in the math and science portions, but utterly failed the others. He would be allowed, however, to retake the exams in a year.

A fortuitous recommendation from the ETH director led him to a school in the village of Aarau that was perfect for him. Finally, he had freedom to study, learn, and dream in a way that suited his mind. The school encouraged students to think in visual terms—and to think independently, without rote drills and endless memorization.

Albert was very happy during the year he spent in Aarau, where he lived with a large and supportive family–and had his first girlfriend! His personality seemed to return to its earlier childlike (not childish) roots. In fact, childlike wonder would mark all of his work.

In 1896, at age 17, Albert's persistence paid off, and he was able to enroll at ETH Zurich. He soon found himself in an uncomfortable setting, however. If secondary school had been terrible and school in Aarau idyllic, university was . . . boring. What do bored students do? They skip class, and much goes downhill from there.

One of Albert's main problems seemed to be that the professors at ETH Zurich put too much emphasis on the historical foundations of physics rather than what was actually happening on the frontiers of the science at a particularly momentous time. At schools like ETH, the prevailing belief was that the laws of the universe had been pretty much figured out and that the only challenge left was refining the instruments for measuring things. Meanwhile, theoretical physics with its emphasis on exploring new ideas about the universe using mathematics as the primary tool was beginning to flourish in progressive academic circles.

And so, two years into his four-year course of study, Albert seemingly checked out. He saw little use in going to lectures he considered dull and uninformative and instead began enjoying himself in Zurich's cafés and pubs and partying, as we would say today, with fellow students and members of the city's Bohemian circle. It was not, however, quite the feckless life that it might have seemed to a casual observer, because Einstein made it his business to keep track of the advances being made by Europe's leading physicists. He was learning for himself what ETH Zurich was failing to teach.

★   ★   ★

At the time of his graduation in 1900, Albert's academic performance put him fourth in his class of five, an unusual position for a student who always got the top grades in primary school and, though he hated its regimented style of teaching, at the Gymnasium as well. This performance—as well as his cavalier attitude—meant that recommendations from professors for whatever might be next in his life—further study, a job—were not forthcoming. It would be a long two years before he arrived at the patent office.

Albert's years at ETH (1896–1900) overlapped with those (1898–1902) of Othmar Ammann, who is also profiled in this book. I have no way to prove it, but how intriguing to think that they knew each other. Even though they had different areas of study, perhaps they took some classes together. And maybe they enjoyed extracurricular student life in Zurich together!

In the meantime, there was an extraordinary amount of personal turmoil. For example, the ongoing financial travails of his parents, caused by Hermann's continued business failures, greatly troubled him. But Albert, being essentially unemployed, though he would hold the odd tutoring job here and there, could do little to help them. In addition, there was between father and son the kind of stresses that can emerge even after a happy childhood.

More significantly, he had fallen deeply in love with Mileva Marić, a companion at ETH who had been an excellent student at her technical school in Budapest and was one of only a handful of women university students in all of Switzerland. In the spring of 1901, they vacationed in the Swiss Alps and as can happen, Mileva became pregnant. Besides the fact that Einstein's parents completely disapproved of Mileva (she was older than their son, for one thing), he was unable to support her financially, and so believed that marriage was out of the question.

What happened next the existing records fail to make clear. We know that Mileva returned to her home in Budapest in February 1902 to give birth, but we don't know what happened to the baby girl. Probably put up for adoption, but that is only a guess.

And then . . . strings were pulled by the father of a university friend, and Albert Einstein went to work at the Berne patent office in June 1902. He traveled to his father's deathbed in Milan in October and, in what must have been an excruciating experience given the circumstances, received Hermann's approval to marry Mileva. (His mother Pauline never really came around; there is no indication that he ever told Hermann and Pauline about Mileva's pregnancy.)

Albert and Mileva married in January 1903. Their first son was born the next year (another would be born in 1910). Albert settled well into his new life. He and Mileva were happy together, and they appear to have had enough income for a comfortable life.

Importantly, Einstein found his work compatible with his desire to continue his own research, including that for his doctoral thesis (he was under the informal guidance of a professor at the University of Zurich). He spent eight hours a day at his job, another hour or so to giving private lessons, and then made time for his scientific work.

It would be wrong to think that poring over applications for patents was drudgery. "I enjoy my work at the office very much," he wrote a friend, "because it is uncommonly diversified." In fact, he was so good and quick at his work—he could do a day's worth in two or three hours—that he was able to spend time at his desk developing his own ideas.

After the *annus mirabilis* of 1905, Einstein continued evaluating patent applications for the Federal Office for Intellectual

Property until 1909, when his flourishing reputation led him to a professorship at the University of Zurich. He had been promoted from his low-level clerk's status, and the Federal Office wanted to keep him, but he knew where he wanted to go. The rest, as they say, is history.

Try looking for books by or about Albert Einstein. The titles just keep flowing at you, there are so many. Not to mention papers, articles, journal entries, and now, all that the internet offers. But even with this wealth of biographical and fact-based information, a *novel* gave me the most profound understanding of Einstein after that amazing year of 1905 when he was just 26.

Einstein's Dreams, published in 1993, was the first novel by Alan Lightman, a physicist, nonfiction writer, and professor at MIT. This beautiful book is infused with Einstein's spirit. From the very first paragraph of the prologue, before we even encounter Einstein's name, we know with whom we are dealing. The book's thirty chapters tell stories—solely from the author's imagination, not from the scientist himself—that illuminate Einstein's thought experiments in 1905 and the theories of physics that would occupy him for the rest of his life until his death at age 72 on April 18, 1955, in Princeton, New Jersey.

In three interludes among the chapters, and in the epilogue, Lightman presents just enough biographical information . . . just enough. The book ends with the sense of melancholy that can come from being on the verge of something daunting— great and important, one hopes, but as yet unknown. I've been there; I hope you have too.

Yes, *Einstein's Dreams*, a work of fiction, tells us as much as anything what it was like for young Einstein during that early fertile period while his body was at the Swiss patent office and his mind was riding a beam of light.

6

OTHMAR AMMANN
(Switzerland, United States)

ICONIC NEW YORK CITY BRIDGES—the George Washington, the Triborough, the Throgs Neck, the Verrazzano-Narrows, the Bronx-Whitestone, the Hell Gate, the Goethals, the Queensboro—all products of the imagination and skill of the renowned Swiss-American civil engineer Othmar Ammann. As well, the Walt Whitman in Philadelphia, the Delaware Memorial, and the Sciotoville in Ohio; he consulted on the Golden Gate Bridge. And just to show his versatility, he designed the Lincoln Tunnel.

Certain professions attract certain kinds of people. And certain people gravitate to certain professions. On its face, not a terribly profound observation. But in its essence, it is. A good "fit" between professions and people is something to aspire to; perhaps even a way to promote harmony in our world.

The word "harmony" makes me think of its opposite, "tension." Both had their place in the life and work of Othman Ammann, who was responsible for designing and building some of the most beautiful and important bridges of the twentieth century. His long and fruitful career spanned the years 1902–1965.

I am sure that there was harmony between the profession of engineering and its bridge-building exemplar, Ammann. Everything about Ammann's early life seemed to have directed him naturally, seamlessly, gracefully to his specialty. Such is not the case for everyone, of course; some paths to accomplishment are long, winding, and rocky. Ammann seemed to know what he wanted to do from the beginning. His disciplined character meshed well with engineering, which demands precision and exactitude.

Another facet of the man was his distinct appreciation for art, perhaps a familial trait inherited from his maternal grandfather, a noted Swiss painter of landscapes and a lithographer (two of Ammann's brothers became painters). In Ammann's world, art and science were equally necessary; indeed, harmonious. He expressed his philosophy thusly: "It is a crime to build an ugly bridge."

Similarly: "A great bridge in a great city, although primarily utilitarian in its purpose, should nevertheless be a work of art to which science lends its aid." He further believed that engineers are justified in making a design more expensive "for beauty's sake alone."

With harmony present in the work of Othman Ammann, tension had its place as well. After all, bridges are public works, and political struggles are part and parcel of getting things done in the public realm. Emotional tensions often arise during these struggles and can become destructive if not handled well. Another way to consider "tension" is its engineering sense. Tension is part of the process of assuring that materials hold up under the forces of stress and strain. Tension is desirable and an inherent part of bridge-building. Those cables on the long span suspension bridges that were Ammann's specialty must without fail hold up under tension!

Othmar Hermann Ammann's early story was straightforward; indeed, his entire life and career were that way.

He was born on March 26, 1879, in Schaffhausen, Switzerland, to Emanuel and Emilie Rosa Ammann. His father owned a hat-manufacturing company and hailed from a centuries-long line of doctors, lawyers, and other professionals. Schaffhausen, an ancient and beautiful small town along the Rhine River and

bordered on three sides by Germany, was famous for its Gruben-
mann Bridge, a four-hundred-foot-long covered wooden structure dating from the previous century.

"Young Ammann sketched the bridge often and learned the
rudiments of architecture," according to *The New York Times.*
Do you sense the stirrings of an origin story? Bridges are made
to be crossed; perhaps the boy's pastime turned into the man's
goal: to make it easier to get to the other side of the river.

Talented in mathematics and interested in both architecture
and engineering, Othmar attended a technical high school.
Next, he matriculated at the very prestigious, at that time and
now, "polytechnikum" in Zurich: ETH Zurich (the Swiss Federal Institute of Technology). At ETH, he studied under Wil-
lem Ritter, the era's foremost authority on suspension bridges,
who had traveled in the United States, visiting bridge sites. Dr.
Ritter became enthralled by one particular challenge of the
era—building a bridge over the Hudson River; we will see that
his enthusiasm was infectious.

> What is civil engineering? Quite simply, the design and con-
> struction of public works—bridges, roads, harbors, canals,
> sewer systems, railways, municipal facilities, and more.

After graduating in 1902 with his degree in civil engineering, Ammann worked for two years as a draftsman and an assistant engineer. Inspired by another professor, Karl Hilgard, who
had experience working in the United States as a bridge engineer, he emigrated in 1904, at age 25. He led a sixty-three-year
career in corporate employment, private practice, and the public sector—never retiring from his profession of bridge building.
He died on September 22, 1965.

Praise and accolades for Othmar Ammann—who, by all accounts, shunned the limelight—were legion in his lifetime and

beyond. He was awarded honorary doctorates from the Swiss Federal Institute of Technology, New York University, the Pennsylvania Military Academy, Columbia University, the Brooklyn Polytechnic Institute and Fordham University, and an honorary master of science degree from Yale University. In 1965, he was the first civil engineer to receive the National Medal of Science. He won the first award of merit from the Institute of Consulting Engineers and held an honorary membership in the American Society of Civil Engineers the last dozen years of his life. Numerous projects have attained "landmark" status.

Ammann scholar and Princeton University engineering professor David Billington called him simply, "the leading steel bridge designer of the age." The National Academy of Engineering, of which he was a member, eulogized him as "the master bridge builder of our time" and concluded its obituary as follows: "He will be remembered by all who knew him for his personal attributes of gentle modesty and inspiring humility, which were in marked contrast to the mighty structures he built."

Othmar Ammann came to the United States to advance his study of bridges; I sensed that he might have wanted to bring his knowledge back to Switzerland, but that something compelled him to settle in the New York metropolitan area. It may be that the problems/opportunities he saw in the confluence of bridge-building with economic and civic development in the United States were irresistible.

The development of New York City, for example, relied on having physical connections between and among the island of Manhattan and the boroughs of Staten Island, Brooklyn, Queens, and the Bronx, as well as the state of New Jersey. Designing bridges to surmount the often-foreboding bodies of water surrounding Manhattan would have been an exciting challenge for any young engineer. (Hell Gate, for example, a strait in the East River between Manhattan and Queens that two of Ammann's bridges cross, is aptly named.)

When he arrived in the United States, he worked first for the Joseph Meyer engineering firm, focusing on railroad bridges. In 1905, he joined the Pennsylvania Steel Company. His assignment in the investigation of the 1907 collapse of the Quebec Bridge over the St. Lawrence River brought the young engineer attention and acclaim. His supervisor at the steel company, F. C. Kunz, went on to form his own engineering firm in Philadelphia and brought Ammann to work for him, from 1909 to 1912.

Any bridge failure is terrible, but the story of the Quebec Bridge is particularly sad. The first collapse, during construction in 1907, killed seventy-five workers. A second accident took place in 1916 during rebuilding; this time thirteen workers fell into the river and died. The cantilever bridge finally opened in 1919 and is now a Canadian National Historic Site. The initial 1907 failure had many technical reasons, which Ammann explained well in his report, but at its core was the human error of "loose and inefficient supervision of all parts of the work." A good lesson for any young engineer, and not a mistake that Othmar Ammann would ever make.

Ammann's imagination became more and more engaged with a problem that had occupied Dr. Ritter, his mentor at the ETH Zurich: the construction of very long span suspension bridges. The opportunity ripe for the picking involved a crossing between Manhattan and New Jersey, across the mighty Hudson River. The technical challenges were immense, the political challenges equally so, but the payoff in terms of facilitating economic development was also immense.

The eventual result would be the George Washington Bridge, called "the most influential twentieth-century suspension span" by *National Geographic*. David Brown, in *Bridges*, wrote that "nearly everything about the structure redefined the state-of-the-art of suspension bridge construction." If you have ever been stuck in a traffic jam on its approaches, you might curse it, but that bridge is a visual and engineering work of art. For Ammann, the achievement would be years in the future, but he was assiduously laying the groundwork . . . for getting to the other side of the Hudson River.

Thus, in 1912, Ammann joined the firm of Gustav Lindenthal. There was an immediate need for Ammann's railroad bridge expertise—on the Hell Gate Bridge, built between 1912 and 1917—but what drew Ammann in was the opportunity to work with Lindenthal on early plans for the Hudson crossing. He did so until 1923, when he formed his own independent consultancy and continued laboring on what became his favorite bridge. The George Washington Bridge opened in 1931.

There was an interesting brief interlude in Ammann's time in Lindenthal's employ. In 1914, Ammann—age 35, still a citizen of Switzerland and a lieutenant in its reserves—went back to his homeland, assuming he would be drafted to fight in World War I. Switzerland ultimately declared herself neutral and Ammann spent eighty-one days building fortifications in the Swiss Alps. He then immediately returned to his work in the United States.

Until 1946, he kept up his consultancy and, sometimes simultaneously, was also employed by the Port Authority of New York and the Triborough Bridge and Tunnel Authority, government agencies that were in the bridge-building business.

His involvement with the legendary and powerful Robert Moses, whose influence on New York's political and physical structures is almost immeasurable, was an enduring one, beginning in the 1930s and lasting some thirty years. Never an

elected official, Moses wielded his power as an urban development "czar" from 1924 to 1975, holding positions in many
agencies and commissions simultaneously. His visions for public
works ranged from neighborhood playgrounds to the Lincoln
Center performing arts complex (which Ammann helped design, one of his few non-bridge projects) to parkways, high-
ways, and, of course, bridges.

Moses, a demanding person to put it mildly, no doubt did
not hold back with Ammann, even as he depended on him and
respected him. In 1968, three years after Ammann's death,
Moses spoke at the dedication of Ammann College at the State
University of New York at Stony Brook (which houses the
American repository of Ammann's personal papers; another
archive is in Zurich). He summed up his colleague as "a
dreamer in steel . . . a combination of realist and artist rarely
found in this practical world."

During his years in the Moses orbit, Ammann held engineering responsibilities for close to a dozen major bridges in New
York/New Jersey. Triborough, Henry Hudson, Bayonne, Goethals, Bronx-Whitestone, Marine Parkway, and Outerbridge
Crossing are among the familiar names. He was also involved in
building the Lincoln Tunnel. (Yes, a tunnel, not a bridge—there's
more than one way to get to the other side of the Hudson!)
Public works authorities in other localities across the country
and in Canada sought out his expertise.

And it was almost mandatory that such a man would serve on
the board of engineers for San Francisco's fabled Golden Gate
Bridge, deemed the most beautiful in the world since the day it
opened in 1937.

In 1946, Ammann partnered with Charles Whitney to form
Ammann and Whitney, whose projects included the Throgs
Neck, Verrazzano-Narrows, Delaware Memorial, and Walt
Whitman Bridges. He was associated with the firm until his
death in 1965. Ammann and Whitney is now the U.S. long
span bridge division of the global infrastructure and development firm, Louis Berger.

A quick look at Ammann's personal life. In 1905, he married Lily Wehrli, with whom he had three children; Lily died in 1933. In 1935, he married Klary Noetzli. One of his sons became an engineer and worked at Ammann and Whitney. His other son was an ornithologist. His daughter, a gynecologist, was known to be generous about responding to inquiries from reporters and researchers about her father and his work; she played the role of an informal historian and archivist.

I mentioned earlier that the George Washington Bridge (simply, the GW or the George) was Ammann's favorite. If anyone can love an inanimate object, Ammann loved that bridge, among all his works. Not for its size or mass or length or height, attributes that others prized, but for its sheer beauty.

All his bridges were beautiful, but this one was special to him. Perhaps because the idea, the dream, of crossing the Hudson River had consumed him since he was a young engineer; he would be 52 when the bridge opened in 1931. Even then, his work was not over—he was called back to supervise the construction for the bridge's second (lower) deck, which he had proposed in his initial design and which finally opened thirty-five years after the first deck.

Bridges are not static objects. They are subject to all the laws of physics and nature. Architects and engineers—and construction managers—do not simply walk away from their projects when the traffic first starts flowing. All bridges must be updated and modified over the years to enlarge their carrying capacities and address other modern traffic needs (such as replacing toll booths with electronic toll-collection systems, adding lanes—and perhaps even decks). To Ammann's credit, when the GW needed updating, at hand were his original plans. He was a man of foresight.

The August 28, 1962, opening ceremony for the new deck was covered the next day in *The New York Times* with an affectionate story that spotlighted the concurrent dedication of a commemorative bust of Ammann at the bus station on the New York side of the GW. Having one's statue in a bus station is an unusual honor, to be sure, but Ammann seemed to take it in stride because it involved his beloved bridge. He even told *The New York Times*, "I am so much in love with it, that my wife says I am married to it."

I also want to call attention to another iconic Ammann accomplishment: the Triborough Bridge (now called the Robert F. Kennedy Bridge or, simply, the RFK), which opened in 1936. Nothing is available on Ammann's emotional relationship with that structure, but if a prize were given for audacity in bridge-building, the RFK would win, in my view. Called a "traffic machine," it is a truly *complex* complex of three bridges and many miles of viaducts that connects Queens, the Bronx, and Manhattan. Each of its three bridges is a different style: vertical lift, truss, and suspension.

Let's return to the concepts of harmony and tension that I presented in the beginning of the chapter. They play a huge part in the success of any endeavor that involves more than one person.

Engineering is a profession that relies on teams and groups of people to carry out the work. No one works alone. Harmony must prevail between and among all, at every level, or the resulting tension will be deadly, metaphorically or actually. Remember Ammann's investigation of the collapse of the Quebec Bridge and his finding that "loose and inefficient supervision" was a root cause? Do you think that the poorly supervised construction site high above the St. Lawrence River was a harmonious workplace?

The realm of "public works," to which Ammann was professionally dedicated, invites tension for other reasons, as well— inherent financial and political pressures.

Quality materials are expensive; beautiful quality materials are even more expensive—Ammann insisted on both, even as others on his team dealt with the requisite bond issuance and other methods of project funding. People living in neighborhoods are going to be displaced by "redevelopment," a fig-leaf word that attempts to hide the real pain and dislocation involved—Ammann had to face that reality as he planned and plotted his designs, with others on his team taking the ugly last resort of eminent domain if needed, for example, to clear the vast acreage needed for an approach to a new bridge. Add in the sheer amount of time it takes to accomplish massive projects—two generations essentially for the George Washington Bridge, from very first plans to second-deck opening.

Harmony and tension lead me to a further consideration—the place of ego in large achievements. People who design and make anything that other people will use—such as bridges—must have self-confidence, must believe in themselves. That's "good" and healthy ego. Even having never met the man, I can tell that Othmar Ammann had a good and healthy ego; he would have never survived in his long and challenging career without it. As a fellow engineer once said, "This builder of beautiful bridges was a man of strong convictions." Self-confidence that becomes destructive of others has been poisoned by egotism, whose synonyms include conceit, vainglory, self-importance, pridefulness. I am equally sure that Ammann was not that sort of man. A "Man in the News" item about the GW dedication included this declaration: "He does not decry or belittle his accomplishments but forcefully insists that anyone who would take exclusive credit for bridge designing is an egotist."

What were the qualities that made Othmar Ammann's bridges so beautiful? A brief sampling of answers from his peers:

- The American Society of Civil Engineering: "His penchant for combining graceful symmetry and harmonious proportions with utility and strength began to unfold in his elegant designs, ushering in a new era in bridge design."

- Edward Cohen, a partner in Ammann and Whitney: "He was the enemy of the ornate, the complicated, the extravagant, the ponderous. With simple lines he achieved a cathedral solemnity, a beauty in shadow patterns."
- John Kyle, chief engineer of the New York Port Authority: "He believed in function with truthfulness; simplicity without ornamentation."
- The architect Le Corbusier, speaking about the GW: "It is the most beautiful bridge in the world . . . it brings you happiness, the structure is so pure, so resolute."

7

HELEN KELLER
(United States)

IF I TOLD YOU ABOUT A YOUNG WOMAN, age 24, who was a new college graduate, would you care? What if I told you that, early in her college years, she had already written a bestselling auto-biography? Would that intrigue you? If I told you that she had earned her BA in 1904, a time when few men and even fewer women attended college, would that begin to impress you? And what if I told you that she was the first person with deaf-blindness to earn such a degree?

Yes, this young woman was Helen Keller. Getting to this point in her life was an astonishing accomplishment. Yet she was only beginning. She would go on to live a long, active, heroic, and renowned life, full of radical activism and humani-tarianism. Her contributions to the world were immense. When she died in 1968 at age 87, she was eulogized as "a sym-bol of the indomitable human spirit."

I want to tell you about Helen Keller not so much for what had brought her to this particular point in time, when she was about to embark on her adult life with its multiple achieve-ments, but for *who* had brought her to this point. And invite you to think about the people who helped bring you along.

Helen literally could not have done what she did without the loving and strenuous help of others. I do not negate her own

efforts by saying that she stood on the shoulders of many, starting with her parents, of course, and most notably the woman
whose name is twinned with her own: Annie Sullivan, whom
Helen called simply and honorably, "Teacher."

As a very young child, Helen was rendered deaf-blind by an
illness. After almost five years of coping on their own, her parents hired Annie as a caregiver. The role of tutor would have
been a hopeful stretch. Beyond all expectations, Teacher—vi-
sually impaired herself—would be Helen's center for nearly
fifty years. There are many who believe that every accomplishment of Helen's—including her college education—was
equally Annie's. At the time Annie came to the Kellers she was
21, so this chapter also presents the story of another young
woman on the brink of her life.

Connections are a key part of life. Not the social-climbing
kind of connections, but the human relationships that help us
thrive. As the poet John Donne observed, "No man is an island." As Hillary Clinton popularized, "It takes a village." As
Helen herself wrote in *The Story of My Life*, her college-age autobiography, "Would that I could enrich this sketch with the
names of all who have ministered to my happiness!"

Helen was born on June 27, 1880, in West Tuscumbia, Alabama, deep in the heart of the South. Her father Arthur Keller
was a cousin to Robert E. Lee and had served as a captain in the
Confederate Army; the family had owned slaves before the war.
Arthur became a newspaper publisher and editor. A widower
with two sons, he married Kate Adams, the daughter of a Confederate general, in 1877. Helen was their first born, followed
by a younger brother and sister.

By all accounts Helen was a healthy, normal child. It doesn't
matter for our story, but she was also beautiful, well formed. At
the age of 19 months, she was struck by a then-unnamed illness,
possibly scarlet fever or meningitis. The effects of either of these
diseases can range from mild to extremely virulent, including

death. Helen was spared death, but she was left utterly deaf-blind. This child who had looked and seen—who had listened and heard—was now enveloped in darkness and silence. Permanently so.

Can you imagine? Literally, can you imagine? For yourself, for your child?

Helen's autobiography, which contains sections written by Annie Sullivan and other people important to her development, helps us imagine. Her passages are lyrical; the others' more workaday, but the total picture is riveting. I would quote the entire book if I could, but I can't. Instead, I commend *The Story of My Life* to you.

Her story has been staged too. William Gibson's 1956 play *The Miracle Worker*, a work of imagination rooted in the reality of Helen's autobiography, has been adapted into many award-winning forms over the years (including Broadway, film, and TV). It puts us squarely at Helen's sickbed with Kate and Arthur as they realize what has happened to their daughter. The scene has no dialogue, only their stunned, heartbroken reactions.

"Miracle worker" is what Mark Twain dubbed Annie after he had become an admirer of both Annie and Helen. He encouraged friends to finance Helen's education at Radcliffe.

The human drive to communicate is innate. It is very hard to thwart. Humans *want* to communicate. *How* to communicate—and to do so, effectively—must be learned, just as everything else must be learned. That's what infants and children do in the normal course of development as they interact with the world around them. All of their senses are engaged in this normal but monumental process. Ask any parent how joyful this process is.

In Helen's case, the process was abruptly derailed. She lost two of the primary human senses: sight and hearing. The ability to speak is not a sense, but it is very much based in hearing and sight and therefore imitation, so Helen lost that ability as well. This child who had begun to learn language could still make sounds, but they were largely unrelated to meaning.

Taste, smell, and touch round out the traditional list of human senses. Lately, the sense of proprioception (the awareness of the body in its space) has been "officially" added; there are undoubtedly more to come as we continue to learn about the subtleties of the human body. Helen did not lose these senses.

In her material about Helen included in *The Story of My Life*, Annie mentioned the "great pleasure" young Helen took in smelling (flowers especially) and tasting (not surprisingly, she loved candy and cake). And Annie marveled at the "acuteness and delicacy" of Helen's sense of touch, a notable development in a wild girl who had previously communicated by thrashing and hitting, and who liked to throw and break things.

> If one or more senses are absent, do the other senses develop or work differently, more effectively? Not automatically. Due to the plasticity of the brain, a kind of re-wiring can take place that allows the existing senses to "make up" for what is missing. The key seems to be how the person is able to use whatever sensory information is available. Motivation and determination are vital, and Helen had those qualities in spades.

So Helen did not lose any of her senses beyond sight and hearing. That must have been cold comfort to her parents. They had to figure out a way forward for their child. They had to nurture the other children and grow a family, not just manage a collection of people trying to survive while in service to

Helen's handicaps. How isolating it must have been for all of them! Playwright Gibson presented Helen's mother's lament: "Every day she slips further away. And I don't know how to call her back."

Days of slipping away turned into years. Helen developed into a sturdy and frustrated child who could only flail about and scream to make herself known. The question for her parents was what to do? The answer would be found in their persistence in finding help. The help would come in the person of Annie Sullivan.

Annie Sullivan began life in desperate straits. She was born into poverty on April 14, 1866, in Agawam, Massachusetts, the first of three children to immigrant parents who had fled famine in Ireland. When she was 5, she contracted trachoma, an eye disease that left her partially blind; by the end of her life, she would lose her sight entirely.

When Annie was 8, her mother died of TB and her father abandoned the children. One went to live with an aunt, but Annie and her younger brother were placed in the notoriously abusive Tewksbury almshouse. Within months, her brother was dead, also from TB. For the next six years, until she was 14, Annie was housed with ill and insane inmates or unmarried pregnant women, or at a nearby hospital; she endured numerous unsuccessful operations on her eyes. Even if she had been able to see enough to read and write, there was no education available to her. Survival was all that mattered.

Annie's own gumption finally led her to speak out to officials who came to inspect the horrible conditions at Tewksbury. Somehow aware of the existence of the Perkins School for the Blind in Boston, she begged to be admitted there. She was, in 1880 (coincidentally, the year of Helen's birth).

Finally, Annie was safe. Finally, she received good treatment for her eyes, though the measures were not curative; her vision kept declining, and she was often plagued by eye pain. Finally, she began learning, quickly and well enough that she was named valedictorian of her Perkins class when she graduated at age 20 in 1886.

At Perkins, Annie learned what would be the key to her ability to help Helen Keller: the process of finger-spelling a manual alphabet into the palm of the deaf-blind person's hand. Annie's own "teacher" was Laura Bridgman, a deaf-blind woman who had resided at the school since 1837. As an 8-year-old, Laura had been brought to Perkins by its founder Dr. Samuel Gridley Howe, and never left. Annie and Laura befriended each other and roomed in a cottage on the school's grounds. (I said earlier that Helen stood on the shoulders of many, including Annie. I can also say that Annie stood on Laura Bridgman's shoulders.)

In an uncanny similarity to Helen's story, Laura Bridgman had been rendered deaf-blind at age 2 by scarlet fever. (The disease killed her two older sisters.) When her "case" came to the attention of Dr. Howe, he placed Laura under his protection. His early success educating her brought much attention to the methods he was developing at the Perkins School. Dr. Howe died in 1876, having made financial provisions for Laura to live out her life at the school. She died there at age 59 in 1889; by then, Annie had been with Helen for two years.

Meanwhile, in Alabama, a multistep sequence of serendipitous connections led the desperate Keller parents to Annie Sullivan. Mrs. Keller came across a passage in Charles Dickens's *American Notes* describing the training of the blind Laura Bridgman. That was step one. Step two came when the Kellers learned of a Baltimore eye physician who was interested in helping the blind. They took Helen to him, and he, in turn, sent them to Alexander Graham Bell, the inventor of the telephone and an authority on teaching speech to the deaf. That was step three. What did Helen remember about the visit to Dr. Bell? In her autobiography she wrote, "Child as I was, I at once felt the tenderness and sympathy which endeared Dr. Bell to so many hearts . . . He held me on his knee . . . He understood my signs, and I knew it and loved him at once."

And finally, step four. Arthur Keller wrote to Michael Anagnos, who turned to his recently minted valedictorian, Annie Sullivan, not trained as a teacher but whose "talents are of the highest order," as he said in his recommendation. On March 3, 1887, Annie arrived in Alabama and began her life with Helen. "The most important day I remember in all my life," wrote Helen. Helen and Annie would be together until Annie's death in 1936.

Annie tells us in *The Story of My Life* almost everything we need to know about her arrival at the Keller home, her early days with Helen and the finger-spelling breakthrough of Helen's cognition of the word and the reality of "water."

Despite all of her losses, it is important to know that Helen had not lost her intellect. Given her almost feral behavior, this was not immediately apparent, of course, but Annie was quickly able to harness Helen's senses in service to her intellect. Annie proceeded, by means of her experiences at Perkins, her intuition, her common sense and—yes—her love of Helen, to bring her charge into the world. She could not replace sight and hearing, but she could do so much else. Indeed, under Annie's tutelage and with the enthusiastic support of Helen's family, the girl began to shine.

It was soon evident that for Helen to develop fully, she needed to move beyond the confines of her Alabama home. With Annie always at her side, starting in 1888 she began her formal education in Boston and New York, learning how to read Braille, lip-read (by placing her fingers on the speaker's lips or throat) and speak (though she was difficult to understand).

There were six years at the Perkins School. Two years at schools for the deaf in New York. Four years at a prep school aimed at admitting her to Radcliffe College, then the women's "annex" of all-men's Harvard University. With generous patrons financing the tuition, she entered Radcliffe in 1900. Four years later, "by sheer stubbornness and determination," it was said, she graduated cum laude and Phi Beta Kappa, having majored in German and English.

Earlier, I speculated on how isolating it must have been for Helen's parents in the years before Annie Sullivan. At the same time, how isolating it must have been for the little girl. "My failures to make myself understood were invariably followed by outbursts of passion," as Helen wrote. "I struggled—not that struggling helped matters . . . I generally broke down in tears and physical exhaustion." But her autobiography includes many mentions of being with other children—hugging and kissing them (that sense of touch!)—and her time being educated in Boston and New York included recreation and sports with other young people. Additionally, throughout her entire life, many people in addition to Annie were in Helen's circle—friends, tutors, secretaries, companions, patrons, editors, audiences, and so on. Indeed, it took a village.

Helen's second book, *The World I Live In*, published in 1908 when she was 28, focused on the senses whose power she still wielded, not on her losses. Specific chapter titles include "The Power of Touch," "The Finer Vibrations," "The Hands of Others," and "Smell, the Fallen Angel." In "The Five-Sensed World," she noted—appreciatively—how all five senses work together and link to other people: "It might seem that the five senses would work intelligently together only when resident in the same body. Yet when two or three are left unaided, they reach out for the complements in another body, and find that they yoke easily with the borrowed team."

This woman, whose life could have been so isolated—keep reminding yourself, she could see or hear *nothing*—was instead a model of connection to others, because she allowed herself to understand them.

The word "connection" brings me to words such as "reach" and its close relative "touch," the physical act that connects us, in the most concrete way, with others. For all their handicaps, neither Helen Keller nor Annie Sullivan—nor Laura Bridgman—lost the ability to reach others, to touch them. It was through the touch of finger-spelling that Annie first reached Helen, and it was Laura's touch that brought finger-spelling to Annie. Their connection was beautiful.

8

ELIZABETH KENNY
(Australia)

As I write this chapter, newly developed Covid-19 vaccines are being distributed throughout the world. Elizabeth Kenny was a fascinating and controversial figure in the fight against another terrifying virus—polio, which has plagued humanity since ancient times and reached pandemic proportion in the first half of the twentieth century. Today, thanks to vaccines that became widely available in the 1950s and 1960s, polio has been eradicated in 99 percent of the world.

How well I remember my parents' vigilance over my siblings and me during "polio season" in those pre-vaccination years. No one knew what caused polio; therefore, no one knew how to prevent it. But it was obviously quite contagious, struck mostly young children, and seemed to be prevalent in the summer, especially in what we now call "congregate settings." No swimming in a public pool, no going to movie theaters, no big birthday parties!

Poliomyelitis is a contagious virus that attacks the brain stem or the spinal cord. There is a non-paralytic form of the illness, as well as a more dangerous paralytic form, which "causes nerve injury leading to paralysis, difficulty breathing and sometimes death" (Mayo Clinic). A synonym is "infantile paralysis" because children and young people were more susceptible to the virus than adults.

Prior to the introduction of the Salk and Sabin vaccines in 1955 and 1961, respectively, the only way to manage polio was to treat its symptoms. Patients whose respiration was compromised, because the virus had attacked their diaphragms, often had to depend on breathing machines called "iron lungs" (invented in 1927, precursors of sorts to the ventilators that we all know about because of Covid-19). And the only recourse for many patients with paralysis were bulky and cumbersome metal braces and/or plaster casts, providing a kind of "corral" when painful spasms occurred, coupled with crutches to support the affected limbs or the spine. With the passage of time, it was possible, though not guaranteed, that the injured nerves could heal to some extent. Even so, persistent lifelong effects of diminished lung function and withered, weak limbs were likely.

From a remote part of Australia, in the early part of the twentieth century, emerged Elizabeth Kenny to play her part. She proposed an alternative way to treat paralysis in general. She relied on gentle manipulation of the body's joints, massage of the muscles, and applications of soothing heat to calm spasms and promote nerve healing. These ways came to be codified into the Kenny Method for the treatment of polio specifically. She introduced the Method into other countries, most notably in the United States at the University of Minnesota, which awarded her an eponymous institute in 1942.

The Kenny Method was a signal accomplishment—it brought much-needed compassion to the treatment of a terrible disease. However, its designer often was regarded skeptically. She provoked controversy because she was not part of mainstream medicine. She suffered from the double-edged sword of sexism and elitism in the medical profession. In fact, one of the remarkable things about Elizabeth Kenny was that she was largely self-taught, a woman with no credentials to her name.

In the paragraphs you've just read, I haven't told you anything that isn't true. But as I begin to tell you more about Elizabeth Kenny, be aware that she was very good at storytelling and mythmaking, at advancing her reputation by what we today call "spin." That is, she didn't always tell the truth.

Just as Coco Chanel did, Kenny often made things up. Her birthdate, for example, so that she would appear younger than she was, or a nonexistent fiancé who "died in the war." Those examples speak largely to personal psychological needs. But her nonexistent nursing credentials or her exaggerations about the large number of patients she treated and "cured"? Those are more serious self-inventions. She may have plagiarized others' ideas, an even more serious charge.

If all the details of her stories-myths don't hold up to scrutiny, though, does it matter? If Kenny painted a self-portrait that was more pleasing than reality, does it matter? If she wanted to tell her own story the way she wanted it told, does it matter? She helped people; she didn't hurt them. She was compassionate; she brought healing to those who needed it, most especially children. Even though she never took the Hippocratic Oath (which pertains to medical ethics), she seemed to live up to that part we hear quoted so often: "First, do no harm."

As Elizabeth Kenny entered the decade of her twenties, the time frame of this story, there was little indication that she would make any valuable contribution to medicine and the world. There was little indication of anything much at all, besides a hard-scrabble upbringing in the thinly populated and economically distressed Australian bush country. By the end of that decade, however, she would engineer the first of a number of transformational "shifts" in her trajectory. Again, she reminds me of Chanel in her ability to re-invent herself.

* ★ ★

What I will tell you now about Elizabeth Kenny's early life is true, as far as I can tell, but I can't be 100 percent sure. I've checked as much information as I can, but uncertainties remain.

It can be confirmed that Kenny was born in Warialada, New South Wales, on September 20, 1880, though she would later claim 1886. Her mother Mary was Australian born, the descendant of an Irish convict, and her father Michael was an Irish immigrant "free settler" who had arrived in Australia in 1862. Elizabeth was the fifth child of nine, two of whom died in childhood.

Australia's settlement stories are as troubling as those of America, because of the displacement of native peoples, aborigines in this case, by Europeans. Much of the country's ongoing colonization was performed by waves of convicts from Great Britain who then gained their freedom, similar to the practice of indentured servitude in America's early years (and distinct from slavery). New South Wales, Elizabeth Kenny's birthplace, was Australia's first colony, with settlement beginning in 1788.

Gold had been discovered in New South Wales in 1851. Michael was a farm laborer at a time when thirty-five plus years of Gold Rush prosperity were giving way to the major depression of the 1890s, the most severe in Australia's history and linked partly to a long drought. (The Gold Rush ended in 1893.) A steep decline in prices that wool, produce, and other commodities could command was only one of the cataclysmic effects of the depression. In other words, in the time of Elizabeth's childhood, there was not much of a market for what Michael labored to produce; eventually, not much employment either.

In 1893, seeking work, Michael moved the family a few hundred miles north; after living in several places, he was able to buy a small farm near Nobby, Queensland, in 1899. Nobby was so small that it wasn't even reported in the Queensland's census of 1901.

Elizabeth, 19 when her family settled in Nobby, had only a spotty education, with some early years of home-schooling and some classroom exposure. She probably assisted her mother in providing "bush nursing"—informal home or "cottage hospital" nursing for neighbors in rural areas. That experience may have been formative for her future, as was falling from a horse and breaking her wrist. She was treated by a local surgeon, Aeneas McDonnell, and became fascinated with the anatomy books—and the model skeleton—in his clinic. (We will see how Dr. McDonnell played a small part in Elizabeth's future transformation into "Sister Kenny." "Sister," the British term for a highly trained nurse, was an honorific she acquired during World War I; but I'm getting ahead of myself.)

A cottage hospital is a largely obsolete British invention denoting a rural health care setting, outside of the home, where nursing was provided by anyone with rudimentary qualifications. In rural places such as Nobby, many people knew how to care for the "routine" injuries and ailments that presented themselves. There was a constant need for midwifery as well.

As Elizabeth moved through her twenties, life seemed to offer little beyond bush nursing with her mother, and teaching Sunday school and sometimes music as well. Her interest in anatomy had not quite jelled into a calling. She had no desire to marry, one of the few options open to any woman at that time, and so continued to live in Nobby with her parents and some siblings.

★ ★ ★

In 1907, at age 27, Kenny made the first of several major shifts in her life. She left Nobby to travel back to New South Wales and visit her grandmother in the town of Guyra. Potatoes were the dominant crop in that district and, with commodity prices in recovery after the depression of the 1890s, Elizabeth was seized by an idea. She would broker the sale of potatoes between the farms in Guyra and the markets in Brisbane, Queensland! All of a sudden, she had a career, something very unusual for a woman at that time and place. She settled in Guyra and enjoyed some success, earning her own money and gaining independence and, no doubt, confidence.

What did brokering potatoes have to do with Elizabeth Kenny eventually becoming Sister Kenny? Nothing on the surface, except that—and the historical record is a little murky here—during her time in Guyra, she may have also worked in the kitchen of a cottage hospital. Her dormant interest in anatomy emerged and she began volunteering as a nurse and helping midwives. A doctor at the Guyra hospital, perhaps improbably but certainly fortuitously, vouched for her, even though she had no relevant training. She obtained a proper uniform and abruptly left Guyra, returning to Nobby in 1910 to serve people as a nurse. In the best sense, one thing can lead to another.

At age 30, Kenny had made a second major shift in her life, apparently finding her calling. It was then, she later said, that she encountered her first patient suffering from polio. And it was then that the real mythmaking of Elizabeth Kenny began to emerge.

Epidemics and pandemics have always been a part of human life. The earliest recorded pandemic was in 430 B.C. in Greece; probably typhoid, judging by the symptoms. From A.D. 164 through the present day, scores of major disease episodes, some lasting decades or even centuries, have swept the world. Economies, governments, and entire populations have fallen to destruction and death from scourges that include typhoid, smallpox, leprosy, measles, bubonic plague, cholera, many flus, HIV/AIDS, and SARS—and now Covid-19. As knowledge of the causes of diseases has advanced, most diseases—not all, obviously—are either under control or can be managed. Or can be prevented entirely by vaccines. Some diseases have disappeared completely—we think; the bubonic plague went dormant for generations and then re-emerged. And in the endless circle of life, new diseases appear.

As far as occurrences of polio were concerned, cases appeared as far back in time as ancient Egypt. The scientific name poliomyelitis was applied in 1874. Soon thereafter polio began to emerge as an epidemic, one that lasted well into the twentieth century, reaching a peak between 1946 and 1953.

In the United States, the first polio epidemic occurred in 1894 and then again in 1916. The northeastern region around New York City was struck with one of the worst epidemics up to that time, with about 27,000 cases resulting in 6,000 deaths.

My parents must have shared in "the panic that gripped the United States," according to the Smithsonian Institution, "as waves of polio epidemics swept through the country, peaking in 1952 with 58,000 cases."

Today, polio is one of the diseases that have fallen to modern medicine and pharmaceutical advances. For example, "Australia has been officially polio-free since 2000," according to the Australian government's health authority.

Remember Dr. McDonnell, with the fascinating medical library and the skeleton? Kenny reached out to him via telegraph for advice on how to treat her Nobby patient, a boy or a girl (accounts differ) who had symptoms of paralysis that might have indicated polio. He telegraphed back that she should "treat the symptoms." So she did what she might have learned from her mother, or what any adult would do to soothe a child—she applied warm wrappings of cloth to the stiff, sore, and spasmed limbs; she massaged gently. The child was "cured."

One big problem with this story, a problem that might make it a myth: Polio was not a "notifiable" disease in Australia until 1911, meaning that no records were kept prior to that year, and so a case in 1910 in Nobby can't be confirmed. What made Kenny think that the child had polio, since there are other conditions that can cause temporary paralysis? Did Kenny retrofit this episode, turning it into an origin story later on when she was using the Kenny Method to treat patients with identifiable polio?

In any event, Kenny essentially hung out her shingle as a practicing nurse, and people began coming to her for all sorts of care (which she often provided for free, or for "in kind" payments of produce and such). She was soon able to buy/rent/occupy (again, those murky details) a small "private hospital" (a step up from a cottage hospital) that she called St. Canice, in the town of Clifton, near Nobby.

Reality in the form of governmental bureaucracy began to intrude. In 1901, the former collection of colonies had completed a decades-long process of federation, culminated in the formation of the Commonwealth of Australia. The attendant development of authorities, commissions, and so forth, followed, slowly but inexorably. Most relevant for Elizabeth Kenny was the Health Amendment Act of 1911, which required all private hospitals to be registered. At first the registration process was slow and lacking in clarity, but in late 1914 the Queensland Government amended the law to make it more efficient and enforceable.

Kenny must have realized that "the jig was up." Although she never directly claimed to have the education and credentials of a professional nurse, she did self-identify as a "medical and surgical nurse" and advertised that her little hospital offered "certified medical, surgical and midwifery" services. In the days of cottage and private hospitals, that had been good enough, but not anymore. Kenny closed St. Canice, claiming that "the world cataclysm of 1914" meaning the start of World War I "closed that chapter of my life." It is more likely that her decision was provoked by the likelihood of being exposed as an un-qualified nurse.

Kenny shifted again. By mid-1915, armed with a recommendation from Dr. McDonnell, she headed to London for the next chapter of her life. She volunteered as a nurse on the troopships that traveled back and forth between England and Australia throughout World War I, carrying fresh soldiers to battle and returning wounded soldiers home. It was at this time that she became "Sister" Kenny. Whether she was educated or not, registered or not, probably didn't matter to the troops she cared for; her new title may have reflected appreciation and affection more than any professional acknowledgment.

I can't confirm much of Sister Kenny's wartime service, so I'll leave it at that. Post-war, she returned to Australia and spent close to twenty years developing what became the Kenny Method and demonstrating its use in hospitals and clinics throughout the country. It could be seen that the method helped polio patients. What a difficult time it must have been for her, though, as she experienced virulent opposition coupled with growing recognition and acclaim, and then criticism again, in a vicious cycle.

Drawing on the same kind of business acumen that characterized her produce-broker career, Kenny cannily and successfully marketed the "Sylvia Stretcher," a combined gurney/stretcher/transport device for patients who needed to be immobilized, throughout the country. She had invented the device, which she patented in 1927, when she needed to move a young woman named Sylvia, whose legs had been injured in a fall.

Elizabeth Kenny was often a difficult woman. Known for her kindness toward her patients, she could be merciless in her scorn of the "experts" who judged her. As the *Australian Dictionary of Biography* described it, "The strong-willed Kenny, with an obsessional belief in her theory and methods, was opposed by a conservative medical profession whom she mercilessly slated *(British slang for criticized)* and who considered her recommendation to discard immobilization to be criminal."

Despite almost total medical opposition, parental and political pressure with some medical backing compelled the Queensland government to take action. In 1934, clinics to treat long-term poliomyelitis cases were established in two cities, including Brisbane where the clinic immediately attracted both domestic and overseas patients. Kenny clinics in other Queensland cities followed.

The struggle dragged on. In 1937 she traveled to England, where, according to one account, she "shocked English doctors with her recommendations." She returned to Australia and opened a ward at the Brisbane General Hospital. But about the same time a royal commission report prepared by leading Queensland doctors condemned her methods.

A less resilient and determined woman might have given up. But not Sister Kenny. At age 60, with a referral from the Australian government, she arrived in the United States in 1940 to begin yet another chapter of her life. For the next eleven years, she and her work would be centered in Minnesota. Consider just two examples of her stateside reputation: A Gallup poll ranked her second only to Eleanor Roosevelt as the most admired woman in America, and she was voted number one just before her death in 1952. And Congress gave her the honor of free access to the United States without any entry formalities.

President Franklin D. Roosevelt, whom Kenny met, was perhaps the most visible of American polio victims. In 1938, FDR had founded the National Foundation for Infantile Paralysis. After popular singer Eddie Cantor urged his audiences to send dimes to the White House (and 2.9 million dimes soon arrived), the organization's name was changed to the March of Dimes Foundation. To honor FDR after his death the "Mercury" dime was replaced with a new coin bearing his image.

Lest you think that I am casting any aspersions on the Kenny Method because of Sister Kenny's history of exaggeration and omission, or her personality, I am not. It *was* a real method that she applied to many patients in her time at the Mayo Clinic in Rochester and the Sister Kenny Institute in Minneapolis at the University of Minnesota. True, we don't know precisely how many patients, but when the names Alan Alda and Martin Sheen pop up among those children she treated, one pays attention.

Much "hometown" Minnesota attention was lavished on Sister Kenny and her Method. And being the canny public relations practitioner that she was, Kenny turned press attention into part of her actual biography. If it ran in the newspaper, it must be true.

Early in 2020, the *Minneapolis Star-Tribune* published a retrospective on Elizabeth Kenny, looking back from the vantage point of eighty years since her arrival in the city. Calling her work "largely rebuked . . . until she got to Minnesota," the article said, "Kenny was unafraid to call doctors 'dodos' to their faces. Many medical men saw red, but the stubborn woman with the powerful frame succeeded in throwing off the splints and casts that had bound polio victims."

And in a program broadcast in 2002, Minnesota Public Radio said, "A vaccine to stop polio became widely available in 1955. Until then, the Kenny Method was still the best thing going to treat the disease."

When Elizabeth Kenny died at age 72 on November 30, 1952—three years before the first polio vaccine and many years before the near-eradication of the disease—there were still afflicted children and adults who were being soothed by the Kenny Method.

At the end of the day, the Kenny Method helped many sufferers of paralytic polio. It may even have helped lay the groundwork for the practice of physical therapy as we know it today. But as soon as polio vaccines were available, the Method became an arcane relic. It was just not necessary anymore. The Sister Kenny Institute is now part of a consolidated rehabilitation facility.

What should we think of Elizabeth Kenny? That she invented/exaggerated her life . . . that her Method became a flash point in medical history? Both statements are true, but I would like to focus on *these* facts—that she came out of nowhere to do work that no one else had done, that her work was based on compassion, that she bucked the establishment, that she was visionary and persistent. These are lessons for all of us.

9

BRANCH RICKEY AND JACKIE ROBINSON
(United States)

THIS IS A TOUGH CHAPTER TO WRITE.

There should only be satisfaction in sharing with you the story of a major civil rights accomplishment grounded in baseball, a sport that I love. This story is part of American history, something else I love. There should only be satisfaction in relating the story of two men, one Black and one White, who were part of effecting major change in our society.

My satisfaction is tempered by the fact that I am a White man. Some may say that my credentials to tell this story are suspect. At this time of enormous racial unrest in the United States, I want to acknowledge that awkwardness. But I want to do my part to illuminate our country's long and continuing struggle with systemic racism and its many manifestations.

The story of Branch Rickey and Jackie Robinson has already been told many times over the eighty-some years since it happened. It involves a business deal that was simultaneously canny and idealistic, and a true gamble. Interesting, but if that were all, why the need to continue to tell it?

Because it is a story of the defeat of one form of racism. Because it changed sports and our society. Because the racial reckoning taking place in our world today demands that the details of Rickey/Robinson's pioneering civil rights accomplishment remain fresh.

"Everybody" knows what Branch Rickey and Jackie Robinson did, right? Everybody knows that they broke baseball's so-called color line, right? What does that *mean*? In non-baseball terms, it means that they upended their sport's long-standing practice of racial discrimination. The color line prevented Black athletes from playing major league baseball.

Branch Rickey, a White man, was the president and a co-owner of the Brooklyn Dodgers. Jackie Robinson, a Black man, was a rookie first baseman on a Negro Leagues team. In late 1945, the color line cracked when Rickey and Robinson signed a contract that made the Dodgers the first major league team with a Black man on its roster. On April 15, 1947, the line broke. Robinson played his first game as a Dodger that day, thus becoming the first Black man to play on a major league team in the modern era.

When all this happened, Robinson was in his mid-twenties. He was standing on the threshold between his old life, which essentially had dead-ended, and an unknown future. By accepting Rickey's contract, he was bravely taking an irrevocable step. We have the advantage of knowing how it all turned out, but just imagine the emotions and thoughts that must have consumed Robinson.

When all this happened, Rickey was in his mid-sixties. Unlike his rookie player, Rickey was an established success. Sure, he was taking a chance, but he wasn't trading in his previous life. The question is—where had Rickey been in his mid-twenties? Pretty much up a creek in a canoe with no paddle, so to speak, just as Robinson was when he met Rickey. In other words, twenty-something nobodies.

When they were in their mid-twenties, who would have known—including them—what they would go on to accomplish? The question can be asked of all of us, at any age but especially in our youth; another reason their story is so relevant and belongs in this book.

Let's look at some background. Then I'll tell you about creeks and canoes and the lack of paddles—the salient details of these men's lives before they intersected.

The "color line" or "color barrier" in baseball was in effect from 1887 to 1945. The terms are usually accompanied by the descriptive words "so-called" and "gentlemen's agreement." This is because there was no actual *law* that excluded Black players the way Jim Crow laws in mostly southern states excluded Black people, often violently or demeaningly, from many other facets of American life for many years. There was no official baseball policy that supported such discrimination. But the unofficial practice was built into the sport, obvious to anyone who looked. As was the case in American life in general, even in states without specific Jim Crow laws.

The baseball color line was a "bright line" that no one would cross. People of like minds (those "gentlemen") could agree to observe it without even having to say a word; a knowing look and a wink would suffice. The color line's intent was blatantly racist. It applied only to Black athletes. Other athletes "of color" were not affected. Branch Rickey and Jackie Robinson knew all about this.

Baseball had been thriving in American life since the early 1800s, with loosely formed clubs and groups of men and boys playing the sport on sandlots and other flat empty spaces, often just according to rules that they made up along the way. As the game "grew up" and grew more popular after the Civil War, organized teams and leagues were formed. Black athletes began to appear on such professional rosters in the early 1880s. But in that era of resurgent post-war discrimination, Black athletes were soon made to pay a price. By 1887, the color line was firmly in place.

Anyone who is thwarted from pursuing their passion will find another way. Thus it was with Black athletes and baseball and the color line. The Negro Leagues developed in the 1920s and lasted almost forty years. It comprised teams playing in a number of small leagues in small locales around the country, though primarily in the Midwest. The teams and their players became both a notorious and a romanticized part of twentieth-century American life. Jackie Robinson had just begun playing on one such team when Branch Rickey scouted and signed him in 1945. With the color line definitively broken and other players signing on to one major league team after another (it took fourteen years for every roster to have Black players), the Negro Leagues system became less relevant. By 1960 it had dissolved, though it lives on in American and baseball history, and in many people's personal histories.

In early 1945, Branch Rickey formed his own league, semi-affiliated with the established Negro Leagues. He already harbored the intent to integrate the Dodgers, so ostensibly his league's purpose was to improve his ability to scout Black players. Many were suspicious of Rickey's real motives. The league existed in name only, never played a game, and disappeared once Jackie Robinson was signed.

Baseball was not the only sport with such a discriminatory practice. The line in professional football was broken in 1946 by Black players who had been teammates of Robinson's in college.

Now, about "Jim Crow," a term of ridicule directed at Black people. The insulting moniker was applied to the system of discriminatory laws in effect mostly in the post-Reconstruction southern United States from the late nineteenth century until enforcement ended in 1965; the legacy of this system still exists, as we know. The laws affected every aspect of any Black person's life, from where they could live and how difficult it might be to vote, down to the minutiae of where they could eat or have a drink of water, to where they could sit on a bus. The baseball color line was not an explicit part of the Jim Crow system, but it lived safely within the system until Rickey and Robinson came along.

The color line and Jim Crow are but two examples of what we now recognize as systemic racism, a Hydra-headed monster that requires constant attention to combat.

Before I use some of Jackie Robinson's own words to tell you where he was at age 26, when he met Branch Rickey and his life changed, let me tell you a poignant fact. That young man was at the mid-point of his life. He died at age 53 from a heart attack. A contributing factor was diabetes, which had partially blinded him; heart disease and diabetes remain tragically common health issues among Black men and women.

Robinson came of age as the Baby Boomer demographic took over from the war years. At that time of generational shift, he was experiencing his own personal shift, beginning to play Negro Leagues baseball after years of prep as a footballer. He was deeply unhappy. But he had needed a job, and his attempts to establish a football career had been thwarted. In his autobiography *I Never Had It Made* (published in 1972), he recalled: "The Black press, some liberal sportswriters, and even a few politicians were banging away at those Jim Crow barriers in baseball. I never expected the walls to come tumbling down in my lifetime. I began to wonder why I should dedicate my life to a career where the boundaries were set by racial discrimination."

And then he met Branch Rickey, whom he knew only by reputation. We, of course, know that both men were on the cusp of forever making their names synonymous with advancing civil rights. All that Robinson knew was that he had not yet tasted any real success. His life was both complex and simple because, as he wrote elsewhere in his autobiography, "I am a Black man in a White world."

In an essay in the *New York Times Book Review*, historian Jon Meacham reflected on the relevance of Robinson's book and accomplishments today, as well as Robinson's difficult role of being "a secular saint, revered for his skill and bravery in making what was known as the noble experiment of desegregating baseball." He recommended *I Never Had It Made* for its "compelling testimony about the realities of being Black in America" from an author whose "memoir is an illuminating meditation on racism not only in the national pastime but in the nation itself."

Jack Roosevelt Robinson was born on January 31, 1919, on a plantation outside Cairo, Georgia. (His middle name honored Teddy Roosevelt, who had died weeks earlier.) The grandson of a slave, he was the youngest child in a sharecropper's family of four boys and one girl. His father Jerry abandoned the family soon after Jackie's birth. In 1920 his mother Mallie took her five children by train across the country to Pasadena, California, where there were relatives.

In that community, whose relative affluence the family did not share, Mallie worked as a domestic. She took on odd jobs and kept her children together and thriving. Their particular neighborhood had few diversions beyond the gangs that initially attracted the young Jackie. He learned early how to cope with verbal racial slurs from White kids—throw a different kind of verbal racial slur right back at them. There was some fighting too. As Jimmy Breslin wrote in his biography *Branch Rickey*: "Jackie Robinson came up moody and combative on the streets of Pasadena. The cops actively disliked him. He had a mouth."

The combined efforts of wise older brothers, a strong mother, and a dedicated pastor (because of whom Jackie not only attended Sunday school, but taught it) largely gave Jackie the support to move forward, though he would be known for his temper throughout his life.

In high school, with the encouragement of his brothers, Jackie

took easily to sports. He was a highly talented athlete. He let-
tered in football, basketball, track, and baseball, and won accolades for his skills. He also played tennis and was the junior
boy's singles champion in the annual Pacific Coast Negro Tennis Tournament in 1936.

> The summer of 1936 was quite a time for the Robinsons. I
> can't resist telling you that brother Mack (who had a heart mur-
> mur, by the way) won a silver medal in track at the 1936 Sum-
> mer Olympics in Berlin. I really can't resist telling you that he
> was four-tenths of a second behind Jesse Owens in that event.

Jackie continued his path of education and athletic achievement at Pasadena Junior College, though two significant blows
fell upon him. In an incident that foreshadowed his lifelong an-
tipathy toward racially tinged authority and mistreatment, he was
arrested in a dispute involving another young Black man; this was
not Jackie's first such run-in with police. Jackie was given a two-
year suspended sentence. The second blow was the car-crash
death of his brother Frank, to whom he was especially close.

After graduating junior college, Jackie enrolled at UCLA,
probably for the emotional support of being near Frank's family
in Los Angeles, but also for its athletic program. There he continued to play, and letter in, those four big sports of his, though
football soon dominated. Significantly, he was one of four
Black players on the Bruins 1939 football team, making this
team the most integrated in all of college football.

> Those three UCLA teammates were Woody Strode, Kenny
> Washington, and Ray Bartlett, all of whom also went on to
> significant futures in athletics and otherwise. Imagine having
> been in that locker room!

After two years at UCLA, Jackie took an unsparing look at his future. He was concerned about his mother as well because, as he later wrote, "I was convinced that no amount of education would help a Black man get a job . . . I could see no future staying at college, no real future in athletics."

After leaving UCLA, he briefly was an assistant athletic director for a government program, then in the fall of 1941 went to Honolulu for a few months. He worked for a construction company and played on the weekends for a racially integrated semi-pro football team.

Jackie left Hawaii on December 5, 1941. He was on a ship, two days out in the Pacific and headed back to California where he planned to join another football team, when Pearl Harbor was bombed. Being drafted was an immediate possibility, and like almost all men in those days, he was willing to do his part.

In early 1942, at age 23, with his fledgling football career over, Jackie was drafted into the army and assigned to a segregated unit at Fort Riley, Kansas. One of his assignments was "morale officer," and he was soon intervening in Jim Crow–type incidents. Most of his interventions did result in changes to the way Black soldiers were treated, but Robinson's ability to "blow his top" became well known.

The very kind of racist authority that Jackie detested was ever-present, but really reared its head when Jackie sought advancement in the army. He and several of his fellow Black soldiers applied for, and passed all the tests for, the supposedly race-neutral Officer Candidate School. "It was then," he wrote, "that I received my first lesson about the fate of a Black man in a Jim Crow Army." Months and months of delay ensued before they were allowed to start school; it took the influence of Joe Louis, the heavyweight boxing champion who was also stationed at Fort Riley, to break the logjam.

Jackie completed OCS in January 1943. He received his commission to the 761st Tank Battalion, which would become the first Black tank unit to serve in the war, and was transferred to Fort Hood, Texas, for further training.

And there he ran directly into more conflicts involving race and the authorities, including one that almost pulled him under. There's another way to look at what happened: It was part of the process of resisting systemic racism that toughened him for what he would face as a Brooklyn Dodger. Let me take you to Fort Hood in July 1944 and give you an outline of what happened:

- Jackie is riding on a bus. He is sitting next to a White woman he knows. He is then confronted with his own "move to the back of the bus" moment, just as his fellow soldiers Joe Louis and Ray Robinson previously had. Because their popular status as boxers lent them visibility, the publicity surrounding their refusal to do so had caused the army to ban discrimination on vehicles operating on its bases. Even so, the bus driver orders Jackie to move to the back of the bus. Jackie refuses. When the bus reaches the end of the line, the MPs are called in and Jackie is arrested after a confrontation.
- This results in a recommendation by the arresting officer for his court-martial. The commander of Jackie's battalion refuses to agree to the recommendation.
- Then Jackie is, in essence, railroaded—transferred to a different battalion whose commander has no problem court-martialing him for multiple offenses, not all of which he has committed. Charges are reduced, though, and he is acquitted by an all-White panel the next month.
- But in the space of that month, Jackie's future is short-circuited again. His former battalion is already on its way to Europe and he never sees combat, serving the rest of his enlistment at Camp Breckinridge, Kentucky. He receives an honorable discharge in November 1944. Jackie is 25.

While he was waiting for his discharge at Camp Breckin-ridge, coaching other soldiers and no doubt pondering a future that seemed bleak, Jackie was introduced to the owner of the Negro League team in Kansas City. Offered a position, Jackie took a chance and accepted. Though it was a baseball team, when he had previously been so directed toward a football career, he must have wanted to stop casting about. After all, what did he have to lose? In his first season, he came to Branch Rickey's attention. Maybe the tide was turning, and he actually did have a paddle in his canoe on that proverbial creek.

I want to pause here and fill in Jackie Robinson's story with another very important personal detail: his wife Rachel Isum Robinson, whom he met at UCLA and married in 1946. She was educated as a nurse and pursued her own demanding career in psychiatric nursing, including as a professor at the Yale School of Medicine, along with fighting racism as strongly as Jackie did.

In the years before they married, they endured many of the usual ups and downs experienced by couples trying to figure out their future together. One of their uncertainties had been solved in November 1944 when joining the Negro Leagues gave Jackie some financial stability.

According to Jimmy Breslin's *Branch Rickey*, Robinson's soon-to-be-boss helped him take the next step:

"Do you have a girl?" Rickey asked.

"I think so."

"What do you mean 'I think so'?"

"Baseball keeps me away so much I don't know if she's still waiting for me."

"Do you love her?"

"I love her very much."

"Marry her."

As a man with his own happy and long-standing marriage—and also as a clear-eyed businessman—Rickey knew that Rachel would give Jackie the support and stability he would need to survive the challenge of breaking the baseball color line. It is safe to say that she was essential to the success of the challenge.

Branch Rickey was 66 years old when he identified and then signed Jackie Robinson to the Dodgers. The team president and co-owner was in the prime of his life, in baseball and otherwise. He was prosperous and powerful. Full of confidence in himself, his ideas and plans. A man of contradictions who had earned staunch allies and bitter enemies. He knew every aspect of both the game and the business of baseball—playing in his youth, followed by coaching, management, and ownership. His innovations in the sport were astonishing.

In 1945, when he met Jackie Robinson and considered the younger man who was risking so much, what did Rickey remember about himself forty years earlier, when he was in his mid-twenties? Almost all that he had going for himself back then—the years 1906–1909 in particular—was that, to borrow and adjust Robinson's words, "he was a White man in a White world."

He *was* college-educated, and he *was* newly and happily married. Certainly, major satisfactions. But an injured throwing arm had ended his nascent major league career as a catcher and he would soon contract tuberculosis, dangerous in any era but especially then, responsible for 10 percent of American deaths. Who, aside from his wife Jane, would have ascribed any future achievement to him?

Rewinding Rickey's story to its beginning, we find that Wesley Branch Rickey was born on December 20, 1881, in the remote farming community of Portsmouth, Ohio. His family was devout Methodist, common in that part of the country. In fact, he was named for John Wesley, the Anglican founder of the Methodist revivalist movement that spread from England to the United States in the eighteenth century. His middle name was a Gospel reference—think of John 15:5 and the words of Jesus to his disciples: "I am the vine, and you are the branches."

On any farm, the labor of strong sons is invaluable. Young Branch, his older brother Orla, and their younger brother Frank worked side by side with their father Frank throughout their childhoods. It was difficult work in many ways. Branch's formal education was essentially nonexistent, with only a few years in tiny grade schools with a handful of other students and no high school at all.

But among the father's strengths was his ability to model the love of reading for his sons; lack of money did not keep him from scouring the countryside for any and all books he could find and bring home. This in an environment where many neighbors could not read or write. Reading made Branch self-educated in the same way it had done for Abraham Lincoln. You'll recall that Lincoln famously pored over his books by firelight and recited lessons to himself while he plowed *his* father's fields. (The fact that Frank Sr. objected to Branch eventually leaving the farm to go to college is a little surprising, yet not—farmers need their farmhands.)

Among the tenets of faith that Branch's mother instilled in her family was the pre-eminence of the Christian Sabbath. When Branch began his baseball career, she made him promise not to play on Sundays, a prohibition that cost Rickey several jobs but that he continued to observe. When he stopped being a player and became a front-office guy, he would not even enter a ballpark on Sunday. This fact was included in his obituary in *The New York Times*, along with the related fact that he "was seldom known to say anything stronger than his famous 'Judas Priest.'"

Some believed that Rickey's "never on Sunday" stance was hypocritical and viewed it with cynicism. Roger Kahn, in *Rickey and Robinson*, gives this slant to the religiosity in Rickey's makeup, along with a hint of the "business" side of the man; remember that baseball is not just a game: "Rickey was a greed-driven man, obsessed across the nine decades of a remarkable life with amassing and guarding a personal fortune. He never once went to a ballpark on Sunday . . . [but that] did not prevent him from banking the gate receipts of Sunday games."

Interestingly, Branch—a shy boy—was a stutterer; we have all been sensitized to that condition by prominent people with the same condition, but it remains a tough stigma to fight. Branch was "cured," tutored by a student teacher from Ohio Wesleyan.

That young teacher's example may have been part of what led Branch to Ohio Wesleyan for college, graduating in 1904 at age 23. The school's obvious Methodist affiliation, which continues to this day, may have been another part of the attraction to a young man steeped in that tradition. But certainly, a factor was the presence at a college in a nearby town of Jane Moulton, the young woman he loved; they would marry in 1906.

As soon as he started college, it was painfully evident that Branch knew little about much of anything because of his deficient schooling. A professor of Latin recognized his potential— Branch *was* a very quick student—and took him under his wing. Thus, in spite of a shaky start at Ohio Wesleyan, Branch needed only the normal four years to earn his BA.

During college and beyond, Branch demonstrated what became a characteristic of his, what today we call "multitasking." As Andy McCue's essay on the Society for American Baseball Research website says, "For the next decade, Rickey's life was a welter of sporadic academics, sports and, eventually, coaching."

He played on the school's baseball and football teams—nothing unusual there—and also played baseball and football "for pay" (that is, semi-professionally) for two clubs in Ohio and

Iowa. The year he graduated from college and for one year afterward, he coached baseball, football, and basketball at Allegheny College in Pennsylvania, where he also taught Shakespeare and English and served as athletic director.

In 1905, at age 24, Rickey made his professional baseball debut as a catcher with the St. Louis Browns; he threw right-handed and batted left-handed. No more than a mid-level player, he was traded two years later to the New York Highlanders (precursor to the New York Yankees, hated rival of the Dodgers). After he injured his throwing arm, his playing days were soon behind him. He and Jane returned to Ohio where he held a variety of jobs. In 1908, he would be stricken with tuberculosis, necessitating a long convalescence at the famed Saranac Lake, New York, sanatorium.

Obviously, he did recover. Legend has it that he celebrated by lighting up what may have been the first of the cigars that became part of his popular image. (Those poor new TB-free lungs!) He entered law school at Ann Arbor, Michigan, in 1910 at age 29. Near the top of his class, he earned his degree three years later, multitasking all the while by coaching the school's baseball team and amassing a 68-32-4 record. His legal career ended after he lost his first case, which was also his *only* case.

And then life began to jell for Rickey.

After his short-lived legal career, he began another career, the one that would occupy the rest of his life. There was a long pause for his World War I service in France as a major in the U.S. Army's newly constituted Chemical Warfare Service (the unit he commanded included Ty Cobb and Christy Mathewson). Rickey had enlisted at age 36, a full dozen years older than the average enlistee. (Perhaps his greatest wartime success was to escape dying of the Spanish flu—more than one hundred of his transport shipmates suffered that fate—though he did develop pneumonia.) After the war, Rickey plunged headlong back into his long and sharp-elbowed baseball career, full of complexity, innovations, and success, whose crown jewel was his forever famous collaboration with Jackie Robinson.

Branch Rickey played baseball well enough to earn four lines in an encyclopedia of the sport's statistics, but dominated front office operations, for which he was elected (posthumously) to the Hall of Fame in 1967. Even before his pioneering work with Robinson, Rickey had already changed the game in many ways. First with the St. Louis Cardinals, then with the Dodgers, and finally with the Pittsburgh Pirates, Rickey saw player development as the key to perennial success. He built the first "farm system," a network of minor league teams that signed and prepared players for the major leagues. He also had a hand in refining player development. Rickey introduced warm-weather spring training sites and many of its teaching elements. The batting cage, batting helmets, sand pits for teaching players how to properly slide, and a batting tee were all among his innovations.

Having brought established Negro Leagues ballplayers to the major leagues—which helped lead to the Dodgers first World Series win in 1955—Rickey turned his attention to identifying undiscovered talent. As general manager of the Pirates, he created a scouting system focused on the Caribbean. One of his Caribbean players, Roberto Clemente, helped the Pirates win the World Series in 1960.

As one of Rickey's obituaries expressed it, "No one in the game made a greater contribution to baseball."

At age 26, Jackie Robinson may not have known it, but Branch Rickey had been looking for him for a long time, maybe ever since he himself had been a young man at Ohio Wesleyan. There he witnessed the distress of a Black player on his baseball team being denied a hotel room when the team had traveled to an away game. Rickey threatened the hotel manager, who was acting under Jim Crow law, and set up an extra cot in his own room for the player. This event may have been a catalyst for the eventual breaking of the color line.

During his years as a baseball executive, Rickey began draw-ing up his own personal plan whose key points were to find the right Black *player* to break the color line, and to find the right Black *person*. Not only did he want and need a talented athlete, but that athlete had to have the requisite character—the guts—to withstand what would be unleashed.

Indeed, when Rickey scouted Robinson, part of the process involved actively grilling him about how he would respond to every type of provocation, from jeering and taunting in the vilest of terms, to pitches aimed at his head. The pitch would be easy, according to Robinson—he would just "duck."

As Robinson wrote in *I Never Had It Made*: "'Mr. Rickey,' I asked, 'are you looking for a Negro who is afraid to fight back?' I will never forget the way he exploded. 'Robinson,' he said, 'I'm looking for a ballplayer with the guts not to fight back.'"

Needless to say, Robinson wasn't the only man who would need guts. The all-powerful sports press regarded Rickey with jaundiced eyes, assuming that his actions were more directed at the Dodgers bottom line than on idealism. Some of the writers didn't spare their vitriol. As Roger Kahn put it in his book *Rickey & Robinson*, "Dick Young, the *Daily News'* most promi-nent and virulent baseball writer, turned on Rickey with a vengeance worthy of Macbeth."

Didn't seem to matter to Rickey. He and Robinson made their deal—and made history.

Playing his entire ten-year career for the Brooklyn Dodgers, Robinson made his mark almost immediately, being named National League Rookie of the Year in 1947. Another per-sonal achievement came two years later when he was named the league's Most Valuable Player. He was also named an All-Star six times over his career. His lifetime batting average was .311. He had started with the Dodgers playing first base, but in his second season switched to second base, the position he retained.

Individual recognition may have helped at contract negotiation time, but it was team success that earned the fans' undying support. Having made the World Series in 1947, 1949, 1952, and 1953 was an accomplishment for a team called "Dem Bums," but each year the Dodgers lost to the crosstown New York Yankees. The breakthrough came in 1955 when they finally beat that team for Brooklyn's only World Series win.

In what is recognized as an on-the-field career highlight, in the eighth inning of the first game of the 1955 World Series, Robinson stole home. He would soon stay home. The team moved to Los Angeles in 1957. Robinson retired. His number—42—retired from the team as well and ultimately from every MLB team. The sentimental number is now worn only once a year in ballparks—on Jackie Robinson Day, April 15, that famous anniversary—by all MLB players, coaches, managers, and umpires.

Jackie Robinson retired from the Brooklyn Dodgers when the team moved to Los Angeles in 1957. He took advantage of his vitality and prominence to embark on an active multifaceted career in business, Republican politics, public speaking, and civil rights activism. The accolades and accomplishments that had accrued to him as a player would continue; for example, when he was named to the Baseball Hall of Fame in 1962 on the first ballot, he was the first Black player to be admitted. He and Rachel had three children. He died in 1972 at age 53; as I write these words in early 2021, Rachel is still living.

One of Robinson's post-retirement ventures was with Chock Full o' Nuts, which New Yorkers of a certain age will remember as lunch counters that were an early version of today's fast-food emporiums. (Oh, those walnut-cream cheese sandwiches!) Plus, any one of the scores of shops in the city were the best places to get a great cup of coffee. (No baristas in those days.) As VP of personnel, Robinson dealt with office stuff in the morning and in the afternoons would drop in on various shops, just checking on things with employees and customers. I ran into him one memorable afternoon at a Chock Full o' Nuts near Grand Central Station. I told him that the wholewheat donuts were the best.

Branch Rickey was forced into retirement after the 1964 baseball season. He was 83 and still quite involved in baseball management, courting controversy all the while. In November the next year, he left a hospital bed to make a speech upon his election to the Missouri Sports Hall of Fame; he assured his doctors that he would return to the hospital after the event. Which he did—having suffered a heart attack in the midst of making his remarks. It was not his first heart attack, but it was his last; he died in early December 1965 with his 84th birthday barely two weeks away. He and Jane had six children; she died in 1971.

As much of a sports fan as I am, I will go out on a limb and make a confession as I end this sports story. I'm oversimplifying something very complex, but here goes:

An aspect of professional sports has always troubled me—the fact that the relationship between a team and its players is expressed in terms of ownership. A professional team is a business, and the people who control it financially therefore own the team's assets. Chief among the team's assets are its players, also known as people. The owners own them.

(I have run, and owned, my communications business for over thirty years. Just as with a sports team, my assets include the people who work for me. Never have I expressed my relationship with my staff, my employees, my colleagues—*anyone* with whom I have worked—as one of ownership.)

What happens to our consideration of team/player ownership if the issue of race is factored in? If the owners are White and the players are Black? Does this sound like a system with another name?

As I said, I know I am oversimplifying a very complex situation. I know that I'll hear from my friends in the professional front offices! I also know that modern labor relations practices have changed the equation in American sports. Yet the kind of ownership system I describe existed when Branch Rickey and Jackie Robinson changed history in baseball and beyond almost eighty years ago. Rickey was the owner and Robinson was the player. Rickey, a White man. Robinson, a Black man.

Rickey and Robinson were and remain true giants in baseball and in life. In this chapter, I wanted to take a fresh look at the event they share in history. I wanted to reframe what they did as a collaboration, not in terms of ownership. The relevance of their story is enormous, given the racial re-reckoning taking place in our world today. Their joint action almost eighty years ago is rightly enshrined as a pioneering civil rights accomplishment.

10

COCO CHANEL
(France)

The headline of her obituary on page one of *The New York Times* on January 11, 1971, was as simple and elegant as her namesake suits: "Chanel, the Couturier, Dead in Paris." She was 87 years old.

I had encountered Coco at the Ritz in Paris the previous fall. She was *the* couturier. That's all one needed to know.

When did *she* know who and what she would be?

That is a deceptively simple question. She *must* have known early, yes? Gabrielle (Coco) Chanel can be seen as one of those influential people whose career, in hindsight, seems to be made up of a number of logical steps, one leading gracefully to the next. In her case, it all culminated in the legendary House of Chanel, founded in Paris in 1910 and the eighth largest fashion brand in the world. As for the woman herself, on *Time* magazine's list of the 100 most influential people of the twentieth century, she is the only fashion designer.

And yet . . . Coco Chanel's story has many twists and turns, ups and downs. I don't think that pursuing—and reaching—the heights of accomplishment as "the couturier" was her goal; rather, couture was a means to an end. "I have been a couturier, by chance," she said, according to Paul Morand's published transcripts of conversations called *The Allure of Chanel.*

I think Chanel's priority in life was survival, starting when she was very young and continuing throughout a very complex life in provincial France, in Paris and beyond. She survived by making fashion not just a part of her life, but her destiny.

Trying to understand Coco Chanel as a person is very difficult. She wanted it that way. She designed her own life. She cut and sewed the pieces of her experiences together. What didn't fit, she altered. What didn't suit her taste, she discarded. An embellishment here, a piece of trim there, a ripped-out seam so she could start over.

What does that metaphor mean in terms of concrete, observable behavior? It means a great deal. Coco Chanel contradicted herself frequently. She told different stories to various people, even close friends and lovers, and then changed the stories and told the new versions to these same people. She practiced "truthiness," a word that didn't exist in her time but that the Merriam-Webster dictionary now defines as "the quality of seeming to be true but not necessarily or actually true according to known facts." She blotted out certain parts of her life as if they never existed—people too. She fibbed about her age when it was convenient to present herself as older or younger—not the worst offense in the world, but a challenge to anyone trying to piece together a timeline of the events of her life. She flat-out *lied* about many things as a way to protect herself, to survive.

Multifaceted media presence Stephen Colbert introduced the term "truthiness" in 2005 on his satirical television show *The Colbert Report*.

On the other hand, trying to understand Coco Chanel as a luxury designer—of fashion, of jewelry, of fragrance, of cosmetics—is pure pleasure. Quite simply, she wanted women to look and feel beautiful. Trying to understand her as a shrewd and calculating businesswoman? Essential. Her influence in shaping a significant segment of twentieth-century culture continues, unabated, in the twenty-first century.

This book's use of the age of 25 (give or take a few years) as the lens to look at significant people is especially appropriate for Coco Chanel. The time period of 1903–1913, when she was age 20–30, is when she grasped hold of her life, wrenched it away from its dismal beginnings, and made it uniquely her own.

"I have never known failure. I have succeeded totally in everything I have undertaken," she told Paul Morand. Shall we take her at her word?

Before turning to that all-important (for her) twenty-something decade, I'll sketch out her earlier years. So many details cannot be confidently sourced. Often, records are lost or incomplete; there is also Chanel's well-known manipulation of the facts of her life. The overall picture that emerges is, in fact, dismal. There's little question of why Chanel would want to cover up, lie, or ignore so much. Shame about her past was clearly a motive.

She was born "illegitimate," in a poorhouse deep in provincial France, and was functionally orphaned at age 11 when her mother died and her father disappeared. She was sent to a girls' orphanage run by Catholic sisters. At age 18, when she had aged out, she boarded in another Catholic institution for girls for a year or two, then was referred to a job as a shop girl and a seamstress; she sang in dance halls and entertained tourists at a spa. By the time she was 20, she was out on her own, living in an attic bedroom. None of this was auspicious or gave any indication of future success.

I'll fill in the sketch a bit, but I can't erase its dismal nature. Born Gabrielle Chanel on August 19, 1883, she was the second child of her parents Jeanne and Albert. They married a year after her birth, under duress from Jeanne's family. Her birth was registered under her father's surname, even though that was not the proper way to proceed. The birth took place in the Catholic poorhouse in the historic Loire Valley town of Saumur where her mother worked as a laundress. Albert was, as he often would be, absent ("traveling" as the baby's birth record noted as explanation for why he wasn't there to sign the register). Indeed, he was an itinerant peddler who often found it convenient to "get out of town." Eventually, there would be four more children, with the last one dying in infancy. The marriage, and therefore the lives of the children, was also itinerant, with Jeanne often following Albert from town to town, either bringing the children or leaving them in the care of others.

When Gabrielle was 11, her frequently ill and always exhausted mother died, of asthma or pneumonia, perhaps TB. Her father split up the children. He dispatched his three young daughters to the notoriously strict Catholic abbey-orphanage in Aubazine, some two hundred miles distant—very far from home—and placed his two young sons with a local farm family as laborers. Albert then disappeared, though he remained present in Gabrielle's psyche.

As if presaging the future, "As a child Coco had imagined a father making his fortune off in America; now she was living out that dream for herself," wrote Rhonda Garelick of Chanel's success years later in the American market. With mother and father now gone, brothers, too, and her own existence precarious, no wonder survival was so important to Gabrielle.

After leaving Aubazine in 1901 at age 18, Gabrielle and, eventually, her two sisters and an aunt, who was the same age as Gabrielle, ended up 150 miles away in Moulins at a Catholic "finishing school"; again, a far distance for girls to go on their own and nowhere near Saumur, if there had been any question of returning there. They were soon liberated from the school, to earn their livings. Never fully happy with the nuns of her teenage years, Gabrielle took at least two things of value from them—she learned practical sewing, and she absorbed the austere beauty of their black and white habits: premonitions of her couture future. Swirling around were various relatives who came and went, not always helpfully.

According to at least one account, Coco Chanel never acquired the skills that are required for complex, ornate sewing; instead she relied on teams of expert seamstresses to turn her concepts into reality. And she never truly mastered the art of sketching her own patterns. In lieu of sketching, she would often drape fabric directly on the models and design from there.

Sewing *trousseaux* and daywear for fashionable women customers and layettes for their babies, as well as tailoring uniforms for soldiers of the army garrison near Moulins—this paid a wage. Social life beckoned as well. Coco, her sisters, and their aunt were attractive young women, living on their own, going to concerts and dance halls with their customers/soldiers. It might have been a heady existence for a while, but the trajectory was not good. As her twenties began, Gabrielle was singing in a cabaret and trying to start a stage career that never materialized; she spent a frustrating season as a waitress in Vichy, pouring the famous waters for tourists. Gabrielle knew she had to take a different direction. And she would seldom refer to this part of her life in the French provinces truthfully.

It was around this time, 1904 or so, that Gabrielle began calling herself Coco. Or rather, she allowed herself to be called Coco, possibly in the spirit of "if you can't beat 'em, join 'em." Characteristically, she then embraced the moniker. What do you think is the origin of the intertwined double-C logo that needs no translation or interpretation, even today, in any language?

There are a couple of origin stories for the name. One that it was her father's nickname for her doesn't ring true. Most biographers believe that the name sprang from the "rowdy" situations where Gabrielle performed. We know one of the songs she regularly sang was *Ko Ko Ri Ko* (the French version of cock-a-doodle-doo) and another was *Qui qu'a vu Coco?* about a girl looking for her lost dog. It may well be that from one song or the other Gabrielle became Coco to her audiences.

Chanel herself admitted that *coco* is short for the French word *coquette*—a woman who is a flirt or perhaps more than that—a *cocotte*. This story gives rise to observations, innuendos, and gossip that would follow her for the rest of her life, that all her success rested upon men, that she was in fact a "kept woman."

Gabrielle Chanel was born during the Belle Époque (1880–1914), a time of great contradictions within French society. There was much prosperity and pursuit of "the good life." At the same time, there existed great poverty and other kinds of social inequality.

One of the many factors of life at that time, not surprisingly because it is a constant fact of life, was prostitution in all its forms. As a young woman leading an unprotected life at the turn of the century, Coco would have been well aware of the hierarchy that existed from glamour to squalor in this intricate sex/money/power system.

Coco was clear-eyed about where she stood in her early twenties and looking ahead. Being a seamstress would not get her anywhere. It was evident that she had no future as a cabaret performer or a glorified cocktail waitress. She had no "background" that would attract a husband to take care of her. But she saw women deriving power, financial support, security, and status by having "relationships" with wealthy men who were not their husbands—was that an option? Being—or having—a mistress was completely acceptable and openly acknowledged in French society. What should she do?

In 1906, when she was 23, a solution materialized in the form of a proposal—no, not that kind—from her very rich (and already married) "special friend" Étienne Balsan. She had met him when he was stationed near Moulins. He had left the army and bought his "dream property," an estate called Royallieu, far from Moulins but only about fifty miles from Paris. Come live there with me, he offered. Coco accepted. Survival was her raison d'être.

Balsan—who by the way already had a mistress living with him at Royallieu when he invited Coco to join him—was determined to turn the estate into a renowned equestrian center, which required a certain kind of social life, one involving aristocrats, fellow horse owners, sportsmen, and the like. Virtuous wives and judgmental older women were not welcome.

Coco—who already knew how to ride horseback, enjoyed the sport (and the wardrobe it entailed) and ultimately became an accomplished rider—embraced life at Royallieu. She absorbed all she could from the *milieu*. She became a sage observer of the kind of women who were the future customers of her eponymous luxury fashion business. She could envision her destiny as being in Paris, perhaps even beyond.

"What the lady friends of Balsan's visitors really wanted to know was where she bought her hats," wrote Axel Madsen. In fact, Coco made her own hats, a skill she had learned from one of the female relatives who had come and gone in her teenage years. Fashionable women began to covet her unique designs— one hat was even seen worn at Longchamp, the society racetrack! Coco became more and more obsessed with designing and making hats, beginning to dream of turning her hobby into a business. Even at this early stage in her career she saw this as a way to avoid the fate of the women she knew who were wholly dependent on men. And she was keenly aware that at any point Balsan might turn away from her for another lover.

Balsan, who had humored and supported her in so many ways, now balked. He thought that hats were an infatuation that would pass. But one of his friends and visitors did respect her dream: another wealthy young man. The Englishman Arthur Capel, known to all as Boy, promised to underwrite her.

At age 25, two years after Coco had arrived at Balsan's Royallieu, she put that part of her life behind her. She left to commence a nine-year affair with Boy Capel and claimed, according to *Chanel: A Woman of Her Own*, that she was never in love with Balsan. By coming to Royallieu she made a decision to depend on him, and she would sometimes admit that she "owed" Balsan a lot. Coco would try to forget the years with Étienne, and, once she became rich and famous, deny them.

Coco had not put Balsan entirely behind, as he relented slightly and, along with Capel, helped finance her new hat venture, located in an apartment in Paris owned by Capel. In 1910, she became a licensed milliner and opened her first boutique. Clothing boutiques followed in the resort communities of Deauville and Biarritz; in 1916, Coco was successful enough to repay her two investors and secure her own credit.

It was at that time, at age 33, that her youth was over, as she later told a biographer. She had gained her independence. She was able to support herself. She could assure her own survival. Three years later, she established her own *maison du couture* in Paris. Not only had she survived, she had arrived.

She had arrived, however, without Boy Capel. He died in a car accident in 1919, the year Coco's *maison* opened. She grieved him deeply, although, like Balsan, he had never been faithful to her, even marrying another woman during their affair. But if she "never" loved Balsan, it was very different regarding Capel: With revisions and embellishments, she would tell the various authors she tried to charm into ghost-writing her autobiography the story of how she met the only man she ever loved.

Coco Chanel continued to design her own life. If survival meant liaisons with famous and influential men rather than marriage with them, so be it; they were liaising with a famous and influential woman. If survival meant making a business deal with a rival, so be it; she would turn the situation to her advantage. If survival meant coming out of retirement in 1954 to revive her stumbling fashion house, so be it; she and it resurged, and she never retired again. If survival meant collaborating with the Nazis—well, the rumors have been confirmed.

Survival also meant what we know today—that Chanel's innovations as fashion designer remain as fresh in retrospect as they were when she introduced them. As all artists do, she took inspiration from everything around her. One early example is especially titillating, her use of jersey as a fabric for women's clothes, starting around World War I. Up until then, jersey was utilitarian, used mostly for men's underwear—how did she know that? What she cared about was that it draped beautifully. Her embrace in the 1950s of a traditional outdoor working-man's fabric, tweed, was less exciting perhaps, but just as significant.

Of all the myriad ways that Chanel changed fashion, her adaptation for women of fabrics and silhouettes (think pants) formerly reserved for men may be the most impactful. Nancy Hass, in *The New York Times*, described Chanel's intersection of fashion and feminism this way: "Liberating women from corsetry—putting them in trouser suits, chemises, short skirts and sporty leisure wear—radically advanced the course of modern feminism. . . . She entirely upended notions of women as decorative and pliant."

Hass spotlighted the Tweed de Chanel high jewelry collection, which was introduced in late 2020. Tweed *jewelry*, you say? I say, evidence that Chanel continues to inspire, some fifty years after her death. The collection uses an interwoven articulation of precious metals and stones to evoke the earthiness of that material . . . the informal, unpretentious warp and weft that captured the renegade designer's imagination so many years ago.

For the last thirty-four of her eighty-seven years, Coco Chanel lived at the luxury Ritz Hotel in Paris, famously entering and exiting by the staff entrance because it was convenient to her office. When the hotel was extensively renovated and re-furbished in 2015, it re-opened with a 2,024-square-foot suite honoring Chanel; the Chanel Au Ritz spa offers her namesake beauty products. One can walk through the Ritz lobby and imagine encountering her—an experience my wife and I once had in reality. Chanel's presence was such that we dared not speak to her, so we stood aside respectfully as she floated by us.

11

GOLDA MEIR
(Israel)

"I WAS SELFISH. I HEARD SOMETHING was going on over there, something was being built, and I said: What? And I won't have a share in it? No. I'm going."

According to biographer Francine Klagsbrun, that's the simple, almost offhand answer Golda Meir gave late in her life when she was asked why she had emigrated from the United States to live on a kibbutz in Palestine in 1921, when she was 23 years old. A quarter of a century later, in 1948, she would be one of the founders of the modern state of Israel; she was issued the new country's first passport. She would spend the next two decades in positions of national leadership. In 1969, she became her country's fourth prime minister, serving until 1974. I was privileged when Shimon Peres, who later served (twice) as prime minister and as Israel's president, introduced me to her in the late 1970s.

You know who Golda Meir was. Can you imagine that she held back from anything? Or that anyone held her back?

Determination was one of the qualities Golda Meir embodied throughout her renowned life. It was a necessary quality in a woman for whom no accomplishment came easily. Not everything about Golda—as she always called herself, eschewing an honorific or her own last name—was admirable, or worth emulating. Indeed, determination, whose synonyms include words such as resolve, purpose, and decidedness, can tip over into stubbornness, inflexibility, and willful disregard for others—into selfishness. Spectacularly, in her life and her career, she both succeeded and failed.

Her complex mixture of qualities was evident in Golda as a child, an adolescent, and a young woman launching into adulthood. Indeed, everything one needed to know about Golda was obvious from the very beginning. It was inevitable that she would become a person of greatness, though I don't think "to be great" was her ambition; rather, her goal was to do all she could to advance the cause of Zionism. Drawing on enormous reservoirs of energy and strength, and seldom fearing controversy, she became an enduring example of visionary political leadership.

"The term 'Zionism' was coined in 1890 by Nathan Birnbaum. Its general definition means the national movement for the return of the Jewish people to their homeland and the resumption of Jewish sovereignty in the Land of Israel. Since the establishment of the State of Israel in 1948, Zionism has come to include the movement for the development of the State of Israel and the protection of the Jewish nation in Israel through support for the Israel Defense Forces. From inception, Zionism advocated tangible as well as spiritual aims. Jews of all persuasions—left, right, religious and secular—formed the Zionist movement and worked together toward its goals. Disagreements in philosophy led to rifts in the Zionist movement over the years, and a number of separate forms emerged." —*Jewish Virtual Library*

Here's the condensed version of how Golda embarked on the road to the Palestinian kibbutz, and her future. She was born into very difficult circumstances in a poor Russian Jewish family that became, like so many others, refugees to the United States just after the turn of the twentieth century. In her case, 1906. In early 1913, when she was nearly 15, she fled from her parents' home in Milwaukee to live with her older married sister in Denver. There she became enlightened, if you will— opened up to a breadth of new thought, including Zionism, unionism, and women's rights that influenced her profoundly. When she returned to Milwaukee a couple of years later, she was deeply committed to Zionism and the idea of a Jewish homeland and was immersed in activism. She had also met her future husband. When they married in 1917, she had already formed the intention of going to Palestine, but they were not able to execute her plan until 1921. After two years, life on the kibbutz had become problematic, and they departed. But her commitment to Zionism was firm, and the rest of her life would center on helping create and lead Israel. Are you ready for the detailed version?

"The 'kibbutz' (Hebrew word for 'communal settlement') is a unique rural community; a society dedicated to mutual aid and social justice; a socioeconomic system based on the principle of joint ownership of property, equality and cooperation of production, consumption and education; the fulfillment of the idea 'from each according to his ability, to each according to his needs'; a home for those who have chosen it. The first kibbutzim [plural of "kibbutz"] were founded in 1909 by young Jewish pioneers, mainly from Eastern Europe, who came not only to reclaim the soil of their ancient homeland, but also to forge a new way of life. Their path was not easy: a hostile environment, inexperience with physical labor, a lack of agricultural know-how, desolate land neglected for centuries, scarcity of water and a shortage of funds were among the difficulties confronting them. Overcoming many hardships, they succeeded in developing thriving communities which have played a dominant role in the establishment and building of the state." —*Jewish Virtual Library*

Golda (called Goldie as a child) Mabovitch was born on May 3, 1898, to Bluma and Moshe Mabovitch in Kiev, Old Russian Empire (later Ukraine). She had an older sister Sheyna and then a younger sister Tzipke, with five other siblings dying in childhood. "In Russia, life was not far from death," wrote Israel Shenker in Golda's *New York Times* obituary. Kiev was a difficult and dreary place and becoming more and more dangerous for Jews.

In 1903, Moshe was once again, or still, failing as a carpenter. Almost penniless and following a path familiar to many, he left for America to find work, first in New York City and then in Milwaukee. His wife and children remained behind, struggling to survive as best as they could. Bluma took her daughters to Pinsk, in Belarus, so they could all live with relatives and await Moshe's return after he had earned some money.

This must have been a difficult time for Bluma. Think of the pressure she was under. Life in Pinsk was no better than it had been in Kiev; in fact, it was becoming worse for Jews. She was living in someone else's home and trying to raise three daughters with little money and not enough food. Essentially, she was a single mother with no idea of when her husband would return. This must have been an equally difficult time for Sheyna, Goldie, and Tzipke as well; children understand much, but they don't understand everything. Later, Golda would talk about the "hunger and fear" that she remembered, of being "always a little too cold outside and a little too empty inside."

The first relationships we have are with our parents and any siblings. These intimate interpersonal connections, whether positive or negative, benign or damaging, are formative. I found much to ponder in the incessant tension that existed between and among Golda, her mother, her father, and her sister Sheyna, who was her elder by nine years and who later sheltered her in Denver. Conflict, love, neglect, and support were always waxing and waning for these four people at all stages of their lives. Misunderstandings led to estrangements that were followed by reconciliations, and then the cycle began again. Poverty, displacement, illness, dashed hopes, anti-Semitism, lack of education, and opportunity—all were contributing factors.

The mother did not believe in schooling for girls, but Sheyna defied her and gained an education for herself. What's more, she tutored Goldie in Yiddish and arithmetic. It was the only schooling Golda had during the years in Kiev and Pinsk.

Life for Jews in Russia during the revolutionary year of 1905 became untenable, with waves of anti-Jewish pogroms engulfing dozens of towns and cities. While there were no pogroms in Pinsk, the authorities were constantly trying to identify what they considered Jewish revolutionaries. It was a terrifying time and Bluma was desperate. "Take us away," she wrote to Moshe. "We can no longer live here."

In early 1906, Bluma and her girls left Pinsk. They made an arduous journey to Belgium and eventually Montreal, finally to Milwaukee. When the family reunited, the shock for all must have been profound. In his three years in America, Moshe had become, well, American. He now called himself Morris outside the family. He no longer looked or dressed as he had in Kiev. As for his reaction to Bluma, Sheyna, Goldie, and Tzipke, he was appalled by their look of Old-World poverty, with their shawls and dark, shabby dresses.

The Americanization of the girls and their mother began, not always easily, even though Milwaukee was accustomed to welcoming immigrants. Learning English was a particular hardship. Bluma and Sheyna resisted Moshe's encouragements to dress differently. Golda and Clara (Tzipke's new name) acclimated better to their new environment.

Moshe was working as a carpenter in a railroad yard, but the family continued to be as penniless as it had been in Russia. At first, all five people lived in one shabby room, then in two rooms with a kitchen; they lacked electricity and indoor plumbing. It fell to Bluma to figure out what to do, so she went into business, first establishing a dairy, then a grocery store.

Moshe disapproved of Bluma's venture and would not help, calling the store "women's work" that was beneath him. Sheyna was appalled, saying, "For this I came to America?" Golda, forced to mind the store when Bluma was off stocking up at the city's wholesale markets, hated doing it. But without the income Bluma's store generated, the family would have remained mired in poverty.

"At age 11, she organized her first public meeting and gave her first public speech, to raise money for school textbooks," according to *The New York Times*. At that time, though tuition was free in public schools such as Golda's, textbooks were not, a great hardship for families such as hers. To raise the money, Golda rallied other girls to form a group called the American Young Sisters' Society that mounted a program of speeches and recitations. They were able to buy fifteen textbooks. Their activities were covered in the *Milwaukee Journal* under the headline "Children Help Poor in School."

What Golda loved about her new life was going to school, required in America for children, a concept Bluma never really accepted. Golda moved easily and well through grade school, graduating in 1912 as valedictorian. Her intention was to go to high school and eventually to teacher's college. Her mother had something different in mind—she wanted Golda to go to secretarial school and get an office job. Moshe agreed. Golda, appalled by the idea, defied her parents and enrolled in high school on September 3, 1912.

Imagine defying your parents for the right to go to *high*

school. What is more easily imagined is the age-old suppression of girls by the people closest to them. Not every girl recognizes that this is happening; not every girl has the ability to try to do something about it. Are you surprised that Golda did?

Let's hit "pause" here and look at Sheyna's life. Her influence on Golda was already strong, and soon became vital. Understanding her will help us understand Golda better, even as their relationship went through the tumult that seemed to characterize so much of Golda's early life.

In 1903, the year Moshe had left for America, a terrible pogrom erupted. Many Jews reacted by fasting—little Goldie and Tzipke among them, but the teenage Sheyna went further. She became active in revolutionary groups; the same ones being targeted in other cities by government pogroms. Both her mother in Pinsk and her father in America disapproved vehemently of her activities, fearing for her safety, but Sheyna's perseverance presaged Golda's. In causing such parental pain, she also foreshadowed the results of Golda's actions in years to come.

When Sheyna came to America as a 17-year-old, she found that being a revolutionary meant something different in America, as conditions for Jews were so different. American reformers were focused on social justice, on building a better society, not overthrowing the government. An additional factor was Sheyna's difficulty in assimilating to American life. Her bold spirit faded. She seemed to withdraw into herself and frequently quarreled with her parents.

She briefly moved away to Chicago to work in a factory, suffered a minor injury that became badly infected, and returned to Milwaukee to the conditions, most notably at home, that had caused her to leave. There was something new, however, to fan the flames of conflict—the arrival of her boyfriend Shamai Korngold from Pinsk. Naturally, Bluma and Moshe disapproved of the young man—partly because he shared in Sheyna's revolutionary activities, partly out of the ever-present oppositional tendencies within the family. Sheyna persisted with the relationship, which was leading to marriage. She and Shamai both worked in factories, learned English together, and attended political meetings.

Then, shockingly but not surprisingly, in 1908 Sheyna was stricken with tuberculosis, a disease that was common among Jewish laborers because of the unhealthy conditions in the shops and factories where they worked.

Sheyna was admitted by the National Jewish Hospital for Consumptives in Denver as a free patient. Only Golda and Shamai were there to see her off on the train—Bluma and Moshe were still too angry with her to show up. Characteristically, Golda kept in touch with Sheyna throughout the several hospitalizations she needed before she began to recover. All along, she had no assistance, financial or otherwise, from her parents.

Shamai arrived in Denver in late 1909 and, against medical advice, they married; the next year they had a daughter. They soon set up the household that over the next few years became a hub of intellectual and political activity. Sheyna and Golda continued to correspond regularly, so Sheyna was well aware of the continued tensions in the family, exacerbated by a difficult economy, Moshe's unemployment, and the faltering of Bluma's store. Soon enough, Golda would seek refuge with Sheyna.

Back in Milwaukee, Golda's defiance of her parents about high school was a short-lived Pyrrhic victory. She may have been determined, but her mother was equally adamant about getting her way, especially regarding Golda's "prospects." She wanted this daughter to marry well and arranged for her to wed a man more than twice her age. Golda reached out to Sheyna, who replied, "Get ready and come to us . . . we have a room and bed ready for you."

Golda got ready. With money that Sheyna sent to her via a friend, she bought a train ticket and, pretending to go to school one morning in early February 1913, went to the train station

instead. She left behind a note for her parents, asking their for-
giveness, but making it clear that she was leaving "so that I can
study." Her only regret was leaving her younger sister behind.

I've already said that Golda became "enlightened" during
her time in Denver. Another word might be "radicalized"—
harsh, but also accurate in describing the seismic shift that she
experienced in her understanding of not only *her* world, but *the*
world. As a teenager, she began her lifelong practice of seeing
everything through the lens of Zionism. She was never a Jew in
the sense of worship or beliefs (in fact, she was an atheist), but
she was a Jew dedicated to establishing Israel as an actual nation.
In Denver, she began hurtling into her destiny. She also attended school.

During her time in Denver, she met her future husband,
Morris Meyerson (later Hebraicized to Meir), a literate, artistic,
and gentle young man who sometimes worked as a sign painter.
His family, too, had its own sad story of fleeing Russia for
America; they had settled in Philadelphia in 1904. Ironically, he
was in Denver as a companion to his half sister, another tuberculosis sufferer.

Perhaps Golda was beginning to enjoy herself, with a stimulating intellectual life and a pleasing personal one. But relations
between the sisters was souring, in yet another iteration of the
Mabovitch family pattern. Sheyna, as strong-willed as her own
mother, was becoming a protective matron herself, now that
she had a daughter. She tried to crack down on Golda's behavior, making their life together impossible. Perhaps Sheyna had
forgotten what it was like to be a teenager trying to find her
place in the world.

In any event, in a crisis move, Golda left Sheyna's home with
literally only the clothes on her back and spent some months on
her own in Denver, working various jobs. She was very lonely,
and when a letter from her father begged her to return to Milwaukee for her mother's sake, she did so in late 1914. She graduated from high school in 1916 and then spent two semesters at

a "normal school" (an archaic term for state-sponsored schools chartered to produce teachers), but it become clear that her love and motivating force was Zionism.

Soon after 16-year-old Golda returned to Milwaukee, she began to embrace the view that Zionism was not just about saving Jews in Russia and elsewhere from poverty, repression, and murderous pogroms. It meant Jews creating a nation of their own, one they would build with their own hands.

Golda heard about the agricultural communities that were being created in Palestine, and as early as the summer of 1915 wrote from Milwaukee to Morris in Denver about the prospects of their joining one of these settlements.

Morris's lack of enthusiasm for the idea paled against his desire for her. When she made moving to Palestine a condition of their marriage, he agreed. They wed in 1917, when she was 19 and he was in his early twenties. Her political work continued unabated. The impression I have of her teenage years, and those of her young marriage, was one of constant motion, mostly forward, sometimes backward, and often circular. Her energy was tremendous, almost exhausting to other people.

World War I and its lingering effects, the Spanish flu pandemic, and many other external events delayed the execution of Golda's plans, but in 1921 they jelled. Accompanied by a large group that included the now reconciled Sheyna, and her daughter (Shamai stayed behind for a time), Golda and Morris arrived in Tel Aviv, on their way to their new home at the Merhavia kibbutz.

Aside from the valuable political foundation Golda laid for herself, life on the kibbutz was personally burdensome. Two years after their arrival, Golda and Morris were gone from Merhavia. It was faltering as a collective, though it would later regain its footing and still exists today. But more importantly, it was failing the couple. Golda was achieving recognition, in circles beyond Merhavia, for her leadership and vision, but Morris was disillusioned and also becoming quite ill.

In an about-face from the way their marriage began, he gave the ultimatum this time. He told Golda, who wanted to have a child, that he would agree only if they left the kibbutz. So they began again, this time in Jerusalem, where their son was born in 1924 and their daughter in 1926. Improbably, Bluma and Moshe, who wanted to be with their two oldest daughters and their three grandchildren, left Milwaukee in 1926 to settle in Israel. (Clara, a college student, stayed in the United States permanently.) In 1928, Golda left Morris in Jerusalem and took their two children with her to Tel Aviv, ostensibly ending the marriage, though there was never an official divorce. She was 30 years old, and close to fifty years of public life lay ahead in the service of her beloved Israel. She died in 1978, four years after retiring as prime minister.

Let me close with Golda's words from the beginning of this chapter:

"I was selfish. I heard something was going on over there, something was being built, and I said: What? And I won't have a share in it? No. I'm going."

Indeed, "something *was* being built," by a very determined woman.

12

ROBERTO MARINHO
(Brazil)

AS SOON AS NEWS SPREAD that communications magnate
Roberto Marinho had died late on the evening of August 6,
2003, play in *futebol* games throughout Brazil ceased. Spon-
taneous moments of silence were observed by players, officials,
and spectators. What should be said about this 98-year-old man,
whose death had the same effect on Brazil's national sport as the
1989 San Francisco Bay area earthquake did on America's
national sport, when baseball's World Series was suspended?

O Globo, the newspaper that was Roberto Marinho's signature media property, announced that night:

> *A televisão brasileira está de luto. A cultura nacional está de
> luto. A imprensa, o jornalismo e o mundo dos homens de
> ideias, de empreendedores que com seu esforço e talento con-
> stroem este país. Todos, pessoas e instituições, que devem de
> alguma maneira seu fortalecimento, sua consolidação, ao
> trabalho do jornalista Roberto Marinho estão de luto esta
> noite.*
>
> (Brazilian television is in mourning. The national
> culture is in mourning. The press, journalism and the
> world of ideas men, entrepreneurs who with their effort
> and talent build this country. Everyone—people and

institutions, who must somehow strengthen and consolidate the work of journalist Roberto Marinho—is in mourning tonight.)

For nearly seventy years, Marinho had dominated print journalism and the radio and television industries, building on the shaky foundation of inheriting—when he was barely into his twenties—the newspaper that his father had founded just weeks before he died. His media properties achieved immense clout in Brazil and beyond, rivaling the status of their American counterparts. His personal wealth, in 2000, was estimated at $6.4 billion.

To tell you the story of how Roberto Marinho came to be so influential and successful, I'll start with his newspaperman father, Irineu Marinho. As the son of such a man myself, I can imagine the energy—and family support—it took to accomplish what Irineu did.

In rapid-fire succession, the salient facts of Irineu's career are these: As a student at the age of 15 in 1891, Irineu founded a branch of a Portuguese royal literature society in his birthplace of Niteroi, Brazil, as well as two newspapers; he became a correspondent for a third newspaper the next year. In 1894, he moved to Rio de Janeiro and continued his career with the established publications *Diario de Noticias, A Tribuna,* and *A Noticia.* In 1903, he married; his first child, Roberto, was born on December 3, 1904 (five additional children would follow). In 1911, he cofounded *A Noite,* the first evening newspaper in Rio de Janeiro. In 1922, he was jailed for four months for helping instigate the *revolta tenentista* of that July. In 1924, he took his family to Europe in search of improved publishing techniques, more sophisticated equipment, and so forth. During his absence, a coup of sorts removed him from *A Noite.* In 1925, he founded *O Globo*—and died of a heart attack in August 1925, less than a month after the first issue of O Globo. He was 49, his son and heir Roberto not quite 21.

Roberto had accompanied his father to Europe. Trained as a joiner and a mechanic and no stranger to hands-on work, Roberto acted as Irineu's secretary during the prospecting trip and then took a job as a cub reporter on the new newspaper.

What was the fledgling reporter to do now? He knew what was expected of him: to fill his father's shoes. Did he want such unexpected journalistic and business responsibility at such a young age? And at a time of personal grief? Clearly, newspaper publishing, a strong work ethic, and entrepreneurship were in Roberto's DNA, but was it enough? As devoted as he may have been to his father, did Roberto have different dreams for his own future that he put aside?

What a push-pull Roberto must have experienced! Many of us have been in a similar situation in our lives. To the young man's credit, he seemed to embrace his destiny, something not everyone can do, or wants to do. Moreover, he was humble about it.

According to a retrospective on his life published in *The Independent*, Marinho "insisted on working his way up from the bottom, learning all aspects of the business." He had been at his father's side the entire time when O Globo was being founded. Now he would step forward and follow in his footsteps, but respectfully, earning his place. A journalist named Eurycles de Mattos was put in the position of editor-in-chief, with Roberto as his secretary. He took that position because of his inexperience, but he treated it as a learning opportunity. And then, in 1931, with the death of de Mattos, Roberto, now 26, took over the position of editor-in-chief.

After 1931, Roberto Marinho never slowed down. He quickly assured some financial security for O Globo by republishing U.S. comics in Portuguese and went on from there.

"A mix of pragmatism and stubbornness helped him build his empire," wrote *The New York Times* in its obituary. The "Brazilian Media Mogul" methodically increased O *Globo*'s circulation, expanded into radio (1954) and television (1965), and, in the five years before his death, founded successful tabloids in Rio and São Paulo. To all that in the late 1960s he added a string of magazines and a publishing house.

But in the long run, it was the Globo television network, known as Rede Globo, that became Marinho's most important enterprise. Rede Globo signed up 113 affiliated stations, extending its reach into every corner of Brazil—according to one analysis, it eventually covered 99.98 percent of the country—making Roberto one of the most influential men in the nation regardless of who the president was.

One key to TV Globo's popularity was its *telenovelas,* well-crafted soap operas that were hits not only in Brazil, but all over the world, including in Britain and the United States. And the network's populist news coverage gained enormous audiences because, Marinho said, it gave Brazilians "a new way of viewing the world."

The son of a man who had been jailed for political reasons, Marinho was as adept as a political operative as he was in business. He had to be, born and coming of age during Brazil's "Old Republic" era (1889–1930) when rapid change in society and in the government seemed to be the only constant. The nation's population increased 162 percent between 1890 and 1930, and as it did so, it became more urbanized and industrialized. The political system was incapable of handling the strains and stresses of these social upheavals, and so finally labor unrest that began in the late 1920s brought about the collapse of the Old Republic in 1930.

As the twentieth century went on, Marinho's political-business acumen came into play during the military coup of 1964, influenced by Radio Globo; in the controversial establishment of TV Globo (which had initially involved foreign investment, contrary to Brazilian law); in TV Globo's coziness with Brazil's military regime; and in the Globo media empire's ability to shape every subsequent national election until the fall of the dictatorship in 1989. Even that was not the end of his influence, according to *The Independent,* "Long after the military returned to their barracks, successive civilian presidents found it advisable to stay on the right side of 'The Journalist,' as Marinho liked to be known."

Not everything Marinho touched turned to gold. Unsuccessful forays into cable TV and the internet in the 1990s drained the group's resources, necessitating a corporate reorganization. And a few years before his death, Marinho divided responsibility for his empire among his three sons; one taking the radio interests, one taking the television interests, one taking over newspapers and publishing.

But the company's impact has remained enormous. Today, according to the corporate website: "Globo is the largest media group in Brazil and controls the leading broadcast television network and the leading pay-TV programmer in Brazil, as well as a diversified group of music content companies." The website adds that Globo has a strong presence in the digital content and multi-platform content distribution business.

Roberto Marinho was thrust into his destiny when he was a very young man. "The Journalist" became successful, controversial, and influential beyond most people's imaginings in a very long and complex career. But by the time he died, perhaps his most important accomplishment was a simple one. He was praised by the country's president, Luiz Inácio Lula da Silva, who had been a longtime, even ferocious critic of Marinho, as "a man who believed in Brazil and spent his life serving it." President da Silva then ordered three days of national mourning.

13

RITA LEVI-MONTALCINI
(Italy)

I AM ALWAYS CHAGRINED WHEN I REALIZE how many successful, accomplished, and acclaimed women face parental opposition in their early years. Often this opposition takes the form of gender-based refusals to educate them, or to relegate them to occupations that are non-threatening to men. The opposition can be cloaked in the aura of care and concern ("I'm doing this for your own good . . ."), but it's wrong just the same. The waste of human talent is a tragedy.

At the same time, I am delighted when I can learn about women who ignored, defied, brushed off, or otherwise overcame that early parental opposition. Hope does spring eternal!

One woman whose story delights me in this way is Rita Levi-Montalcini, the Nobel Prize–winning Italian neurologist who was born in 1909 and died in 2012—yes, at age 103. Much as her father loved her, he refused to allow her to have a career—even to go beyond a high school education. Much as Rita loved her father, she stood up to him. We know who won that argument.

Rita Levi-Montalcini always prevailed. And she always had time for those around her—especially young women and men. I was accustomed to meeting up with her at the Ambrosetti Conference, the famed economic meeting held annually at the Villa d'Este in Como, Italy. One year, my teenage son Peter came with me—and Dr. Levi-Montalcini gave him ten quality minutes of her time, talking to him about his ambitions. Peter has never forgotten that.

Rita was born, with her twin sister Paola, on April 22, 1909, in Turin, an ancient and iconic city along the Po River in northern Italy. Their parents were Adamo Levi, an electrical engineer, mathematician, and factory owner, and Adele Montalcini Levi. Adele was a talented artist, but more importantly for the era, she was also a traditional Italian wife and mother. There was an older sister and brother, Anna and Gino. Adamo was successful in his work, and the well-off family was "filled with love and reciprocal devotion," wrote Dr. Levi-Montalcini in her Nobel Prize autobiography, continuing: "Both parents were highly cultured and instilled in us their high appreciation of intellectual pursuit. It was, however, a typical Victorian style of life, all decisions being taken by the head of the family, the husband and father."

Adamo Levi actually had great respect for women, but he was convinced that pursuing a professional career would interfere with their being good wives and mothers, and so he forbade all three daughters—Anna, Paola, and Rita—to enroll at a university.

Of the other Levi-Montalcini siblings, Anna, who enjoyed writing, emulated their mother by embracing the life of wife and mother. Gino became a prominent architect and a professor at the University of Turin. Rita's twin, Paola, was an outstanding painter with a long and acclaimed career.

Young Rita respected her father, though he also intimidated her. She adored her mother, "an exquisite human being," she said in her Nobel autobiography. After high school, where she had thrived, Rita had no particular direction in mind. She knew only that she did not want "the subordinate role played by the female in a society run entirely by men." She also knew that she did not want to be a wife or a mother, even though those seemed to be the only roles available to her. If she did not embrace those unwanted roles, she later said poignantly, "In my family, I saw that I could never accomplish anything."

But in her heart, Rita actually did know what she wanted: to leave the restricted world in which she had been raised and to escape the narrow expectations of Italian society. She wanted to explore life and realize her potential, whatever it was.

Rita's uncertainty came to an abrupt end in 1929, when she was 20. The family's beloved governess, who had lived with them for many years, died of cancer. Such an event can be paralyzing, or it can be inspiring. Looking for meaning and purpose in the midst of a tremendous personal shock, Rita found her focus—she would become a doctor.

With her mother's encouragement, Rita faced her father. She wrote in her autobiography: "I realized that I could not possibly adjust to a feminine role as conceived by my father and asked his permission to engage in a professional career. He listened, looking at me with that serious and penetrating gaze of his that caused me such trepidation."

I have been the target of such a gaze, and my sons would probably say that they have as well. I know from the point of view of both parent and child, how challenging that conversation must have been. Rita's autobiographical account continued: "He objected that it was a long and difficult course of study, unsuitable for a woman. Since I had finished school three years previously, it would not be easy to take it up again. I assured him that I was not afraid of that."

Maybe Adamo looked, really looked, at his daughter during this conversation and recognized what he was seeing: a brave, confident, and determined young woman. Maybe he listened closely to her. Maybe he accepted that *his* way for Rita was not *her* way for her. Although he may still have disapproved, he agreed to support his daughter. With his reluctant assent, Rita embarked on an independent study program so she could make up the academic background she was lacking. Tutors instructed her in languages, math, and science, and she taught herself philosophy, literature, and history. By the autumn of 1930, she was able to enroll as a medical student at Turin University—she even had the highest score among the home-taught students who took the entrance exam that year. In a class of three hundred, Rita was one of only seven women.

Adamo Levi did not live even to see his daughter graduate from medical school, never mind witness her groundbreaking research and her Nobel achievement. In August 1932, he died of a series of strokes and heart attacks. He was 65 and Rita was 23.

In 1936, at age 27, Dr. Levi-Montalcini graduated summa cum laude and commenced the nerve growth factor research that would define her career. Fifty years later, she was awarded the Nobel Prize in Physiology or Medicine, sharing it with her research partner of thirty plus years, Dr. Stanley Cohen. According to *The New York Times*, the two biochemists "discovered critical chemical tools that the body uses to direct cell growth and build nerve networks, opening the way for the study of how those processes can go wrong in diseases like dementia and cancer." Their work revolutionized the study of neural development, "from how we think about it to how we intervene."

Besides the Victorian-style paternal disapproval that she overcame, Dr. Levi-Montalcini faced a much more dangerous enemy: the forces of anti-Semitism and Fascism in Italy, reflecting the events in Nazi Germany. Mussolini had come to power in 1922, when Rita was barely a teenager. In 1938, tracking Hitler's views of Aryan superiority and applying them to Italy, Mussolini began stripping Jewish citizens of their rights—including those of scientists to pursue their academic careers. Published materials such as "The Manifesto of Race" and "Laws for the Defense of Race" helped fan the flames of anti-Semitism.

Undaunted, but not wanting to expose her non-Jewish colleagues to repercussions, Dr. Levi-Montalcini relocated her research to Belgium. When Hitler's influence metastasized throughout Europe and Belgium was no longer safe, she returned to Italy. There she sheltered with her family, first in Turin and then in Florence, where she set up a secret lab in a bedroom in her home. It was during this time period that she laid the groundwork for her later investigation of the nerve growth factor. "You never know what is good, what is bad in life," she later mused. "I mean, in my case, it was my good chance."

Dr. Giuseppe Levi (no relation), a professor during medical school who had become her mentor there, now assisted her. Using eggs collected from neighboring farmers, they experimented, painstakingly, with chick embryos, learning the secrets of neural development. Their inspiration was Dr. Viktor Hamburger, who was doing similar chick-embryo research in the United States, at Washington University in St. Louis, Missouri. Dr. Levi-Montalcini also worked as a medical doctor at Florence's refugee camps.

> Dr. Giuseppe Levi was a famously rigorous scientist who focused on histology (the microscopic structure of tissue). He was apparently a Nobel-whisperer, as two of Rita's colleagues from her time studying with him in Turin also became Nobel laureates, about a decade earlier than her award.

When World War II ended in 1945, she could once again work openly at the University of Turin. Two years later, she accepted Dr. Hamburger's invitation to join him for a year at Washington University. The temporary assignment turned permanent. She and Dr. Cohen began their collaboration there in the early 1950s. Dr. Levi-Montalcini became an associate professor in 1956 and a full professor in 1958.

She officially retired from the university in 1977, though she remained very active as a guest professor; her obituary in *The Economist* noted that "she never really retired, snapping that it led to decay of the brain." In her "retirement," she continued to lecture widely and publish prolifically. She traveled regularly between St. Louis and Rome, where she had established the Institute of Cell Biology.

Along with her sister Paola, Rita established two foundations to help young people make decisions for their futures. One foundation was dedicated to the memory of their father Adamo. These efforts with young people were a direct result of the prize money—and the celebrity—associated with being a Nobel laureate: "I can do things that are very, very important, which I would never have been able to do if I did not receive it," she told *Scientific American* in 1993. "It has given me the possibility of helping a lot of people."

In addition to the Nobel, her other awards were numerous, including the U.S. National Medal of Science and the Albert Lasker Award for Basic Medical Research. She held honorary degrees from universities in Italy, Spain, and the United States, along with many other academic prizes, and was a Goodwill Ambassador for the United Nations Food and Agriculture Organization. Most interesting of all honors, perhaps, was being named Senator for Life in 2001 by the Italian Senate (she was 92 and would live for another eleven years).

In 2009, at age 100, Dr. Rita Levi-Montalcini declared that, "I have a mind that is superior—thanks to experience—than when I was 20." That year, she was feted at Rome's City Hall for the distinction of being the first Nobel laureate to reach the century mark. She attributed her long life to her "ferocious" work schedule, only five hours of sleep a night and an abstemious diet. Working until the end, she published her final paper three years later. She was 103 when she died on December 30, 2012.

Rita Levi-Montalcini always said that she never regretted her girlhood decision to not marry or have children: "And it was a very good decision—at that time, I could never have done anything in particular if I had married," she told *Scientific American*. I hope that her father would agree, and approve; Rita's professional achievements aside, she lived her own life. And I hope that all young people with questions of marriage, children, and careers can answer them freely, with support and not opposition.

14

EDITH PIAF
(France)

EDITH PIAF INSPIRES ME TO ASK AGE-OLD QUESTIONS. What is the source of beauty? What part do tragedy and sadness play? Do they help us recognize beauty? Are they required to give depth and richness to the experience of beauty, or are they poisons? Do tragedy and sadness make beauty a reality, or do they assure that beauty will remain unattainable?

Knowing even the rudimentary facts of Edith Piaf's life seems to indicate that beauty and misery can co-exist because, for her, they did. It doesn't seem possible that she would have been gifted with an incredibly lovely singing voice, yet she was. We continue to listen to recordings of her performances today, some sixty years after her death, because she showed us that beauty can transcend misery. If she had enjoyed a stable and conventional existence, it may not have been necessary for her to sing; she might have remained forever unknown. And that would not be good.

However it is that you listen to music, put on *Non, je ne regrette rien* or *La vie en Rose* or *Milord*—three of the greatest among the almost three hundred songs in her repertoire—and join me in exploring the life of this mesmerizing *chanteuse*. Did she have any idea what she would achieve, that she would become "a symbol of French passion and tenacity," as one biography has it? That her "gut-wrenching tones would come to represent France to the French and touch listeners all over the world, whether or not they spoke her language," as another has it?

What was her situation at the age—25 or so—that is the pivot point of all the stories in this book: Did she find herself there, or did she put herself there? How much "agency" did she have over her own life?

From a birth rumored to have taken place on the street—literally, on the pavement in a poor and run-down district of Paris—on December 19, 1915, Edith Piaf attained the heights of international fame. An uneducated street urchin became "almost universally regarded as France's greatest popular singer," according to her allmusic.com biography. Her death at age 47 "caused a nationwide outpouring of grief." Tens of thousands of people thronged the streets of Paris to follow her funeral procession; her gravesite was mobbed and remained a tourist destination for years to come.

Whether on the street or in the maternity ward at a nearby hospital, it was a rough start. Named Edith Giovanna Gassion at birth, the little girl may as well have been an orphan, her parents took so little interest in her. They were both street performers: her father Louis, with a background in the theater, was an acrobat and singer; her mother Anita, who came from a circus family, was a singer who also performed in cafés under the name "Line Marsa." Both were eventually alcoholics, Anita a drug addict.

As you read on, keep in mind that much of her past is shrouded in mystery and many of the details may have been fabricated or at least embellished once she became a celebrity. "It is often impossible to separate fact from fiction," wrote Carolyn Burke in *No Regrets: The Life of Edith Piaf.*

With Louis away serving in World War I, Anita essentially abandoned Edith, placing the little girl under the so-called but really nonexistent care of her own mother. Anita continued to pursue her career, which may have included street prostitution. When Louis returned from the war, he took a malnourished Edith to Normandy to live with his mother, who ran a brothel in the town of Bernay. Unexpectedly, there among the prostitutes, Edith experienced some care and kindness, since the women of the house are credited with helping her heal from a long and blinding bout of conjunctivitis. Their prayerful efforts included a pilgrimage to Lisieux, the birthplace of St. Therese, the "Little Flower." Edith regained her eyesight.

At some point, when she was 7 or 9 or 12—no one was really keeping track of the girl—her father reclaimed her, sort of. She took to the streets with him and a half sister as a singer and play-acted as a winsome little girl who would pass the hat for donations from onlookers. No schooling, of course. She traveled all over France and sang for tips in the street, squares, cafés, and military camps, while living in a succession of cheap, squalid hotels. She moved in circles of petty criminals and led a promiscuous nightlife, with a predilection for pimps and other street toughs who could protect her while she earned her meager living as a street performer.

Let's pause here. In our world, this would be abuse. In her world, it was what it was. In 1932, at age 17, Edith gave birth to a daughter, Marcelle. She would treat Marcelle the same way that she had been treated—neglecting her, ignoring her, effectively abandoning her; abuse is often a generational disease, especially if there are no good models to follow. The little girl died at age 2 or 3 of meningitis.

In 1935, around the time of her daughter's death, Edith was discovered as a singer. She was 20 years old and, under the wing of cabaret owner Louis Leplée, she began the process that would turn her into the enduring icon that she is. Leplée saw that she had something, even if *she* didn't quite know it yet.

But she must have recognized what he could offer her: "Fate took me by the hand to turn me into the singer I would become," she acknowledged. "As a girl of the streets, she knew her only chance to transcend them would depend on her determination and talents," wrote biographer Carolyn Burke.

The first thing Leplée did was to give Edith a stage name: "*La Môme Piaf*"—slang for "waif sparrow" or "little sparrow." This was a canny decision on his part. The name certainly fit Edith because she was small (four feet eight inches) and delicate and sang as naturally as any little bird. But the name also conveyed a desirable emotional tone of being insubstantial or inconsequential. The "little sparrow" would evoke sympathy among audiences, who would then be astonished by the power, and the sweetness, of her voice.

It was Leplée's coaching that gave Piaf—as I will call her from now on—her stage presence (which included wearing a distinctive little black dress) and that helped her develop her distinctive *vibrato* and *rubato* and *glissando* delivery techniques. It was Leplée's connections that caused songwriters to clamor for the chance to write for Piaf and drove the publicity process that kept his cabaret full of fans for his newest sensation. Here began the audience appeal that she never lost.

Scandal erupted soon enough, in 1936, when Leplée was murdered and Piaf—who was keeping up a disreputable lifestyle (but what other way did she know?)—was initially suspected of the crime. She was cleared, though mobsters who were her previous associates were found to be responsible and the odor of accusation clung to her. Only a year into the career that Leplée had engineered for her, she could see fans beginning to turn away, and perhaps her future slipping away too.

At age 21, she made her own canny decision. She wouldn't wait for someone to discover her again; she would reach out for the help she needed to survive and to thrive. This became her lifelong pattern. And in a "pay it forward" sort of way, when she became established, she reached out to help others when they were in need.

★   ★   ★

After Leplée's death, Piaf turned to Raymond Asso, a business-man and songwriter. She had earlier rejected one of his songs, though one of her rivals recorded it to great success; she decided she needed him on her side. Asso became her lover as well as her manager, or maybe the other way around. In any event, he immediately began a rehabilitation process that included severing her from all former associates and trying to make up for her almost complete lack of formal education.

Asso also made another shrewd decision. He got Piaf to tell him about her childhood on the streets and her time in a bordello so that he could choose a repertoire of songs that would reflect her experiences. Armed with the insights that Asso had gleaned, many well-known songwriters seized the opportunity to write for her. Who would not want the opportunity to have one's work delivered by that voice . . . that *personality*? For most assuredly, Piaf had magnetism. She was becoming a star.

Piaf was neither a composer nor a lyricist, so she did not create her own material, not in those early days with Asso or in the future. She made choices, though; in a symbiotic creative partnership, she made what others were inspired to give her uniquely her own. She couldn't read music, but she had a sharp ear and a marvelous ability to memorize songs, and as she did so, she made decisions that "served to enhance a song's emotional qualities," according to biographer Burke.

Piaf's "star power" rests on two factors, I believe. The first is her actual voice, whose descriptors include poignant, heartbreaking, and resonant. The second is that, as she sang about her own loves, losses, *tristesse*, and grief, she convinced listeners that she was also singing about *them* and their unique experiences. She turned what could have been generic expressions into ones that were personal to her *and* personal to her listeners.

In the fall of 1939, as Piaf approached her mid-twenties, Asso went off to war and Piaf took a new lover. When that relationship ended, she and her half sister moved into an apartment located over a high-class brothel. This detail is important, because in June 1940, the Nazis, having invaded France, took control of Paris and many of the officers patronized the brothel. It is not far-fetched to assume that these officers, and other leading Nazis, would not only meet Piaf, but also visit the nightclubs, intimate cafés, and large music halls where she performed. They must have been as entranced by her as anyone else would be, and she had to survive.

Thus, began the gossip that would attach to Piaf, that she was overly friendly with the Nazis, perhaps even a collaborator: Her name was placed on "purge panels" set up to call out such people. The other side of that coin was that Piaf is known to have aided Jewish composers and pianists, men who supported her singing career, to escape the occupation; there are additional stories of her low-key resistance to various Nazi demands.

Consider the following story, from the tribute website edithpiaf.com: "Singing for high-ranking Germans . . . earned Edith Piaf the right to pose for photos with French prisoners of war, ostensibly as a morale-boosting exercise. Once in possession of their celebrity photos, prisoners were able to cut out their own images and use them in forged papers as part of escape plans."

One hundred and eighteen prisoners used their fake cards to escape, according to Burke. And after Piaf gave a purge panel the names of Jewish friends whose shelter she had arranged and financed, the panel voted unanimously that she was not to be sanctioned in post-war France and that she deserved congratulations.

Performers like her had been forced to comply with the occupiers' demands. "I forced myself to navigate around the pitfalls of the Nazi propaganda machine to keep the trust of the French public," she explained.

What the truth is, I don't know. Piaf was there first in Paris, and then the Germans arrived; eventually they left, and she was still there. She made the most of a terrible situation. The world was coming to meet Piaf on the very streets that birthed her. I wonder, is it happenstance, or evidence of creative talent and will, to find strength in our origins?

There are many parallels between Edith Piaf and Coco Chanel, another luminous Frenchwoman in this book who had her own intersection with the Nazis. I believe that survival was the impetus that drove both women, and that both Piaf and Chanel did their best to thread the needle of their circumstances. In Chanel's case, survival meant that she reached the heights of accomplishment in the world of fashion and beauty (in the cosmetic sense of the word, which is not to say it is not real). In Piaf's case, survival brought her to the pinnacle of stardom. Both women needed to escape their beginnings, to make the best of the very bad hand that life had dealt them when they were young. And both women needed to try, at least, to be the agents of their own lives, to determine their own fates.

Interestingly, speaking of self-determination, the names by which these women will always be known were given to them by others, and I don't mean their parents; "Coco" named by rowdy audiences in her early days as a cabaret singer in the French hinterlands and "Piaf" named by a cabaret owner in Paris.

When the war ended, Piaf was 30 years old and leading a life that grew more and more complex, with lovers, husbands, friends, and hangers-on, performances, recording sessions, professional patrons, protégés, wealth, stage and film roles, new songwriters to audition, new songs to try out, international travel, and all the other trappings of a spectacular career. She was a *star*.

Loss and sadness come to all of us, of course, but not always tragedy. Piaf became dogged by tragedy, most poignantly the 1949 death of her lover Marcel Cerdan, a middleweight boxing champion who was, at the time, a hero to the French people. Cerdan's plane crashed in the Azores as he was traveling from France to New York to meet up with Piaf. Her devastation included the knowledge that she had persuaded him to fly rather than make the ocean crossing by boat, which plunged her into drug and alcohol abuse.

Piaf would suffer from these addictions, in spite of much treatment, for the rest of her life. She was seriously injured three times in automobile accidents; cancer struck her as well. Even so, her voice never lost its power or its allure. Her career never ended, because she was a survivor. She died at age 47 on October 10, 1963; a singular *chanteuse* who never gave up. She was buried next to her daughter Marcelle.

I used to have the privilege and pleasure of traveling to Paris annually. I always found the opportunity to visit the Montmartre district, where Piaf had gotten her start and where her work was celebrated by virtually everyone. Spending many an evening in one café or another, absorbing the low-lit, smoky, and *liqueur*-tinged atmosphere, I would imagine that I had been there in the time of Piaf. I never met her, as it was not until the mid-1980s, some twenty years after her death, that I discovered her recordings. *Quel dommage.*

Now, as I write this, the world is in the grip of the seemingly intractable coronavirus pandemic. I can't assume when I might ever travel freely again. That's a very trivial concern, of course, but it does bring me some *tristesse.* When that happens, I put on some Piaf and take a look at one of my fondest possessions—a love letter that Marcel Cerdan wrote to Edith Piaf and that I obtained from a collector. I summon up the melancholy that I associate with Piaf, and I ponder the origins of beauty.

15

I. M. PEI
(China, United States)

"THERE IS NO WAY THAT THE FRENCH PEOPLE will stand for it."
François Mitterrand was adamant.

"The French people are always *avant-garde*. They will embrace it." Jacques Chirac was equally certain.

All eyes in the room turned to look at the slight, elegant, bespectacled man who smiled with serene confidence as he stood next to the scale model representing his answer to the professional challenge of a lifetime. The man was the renowned architect I. M. Pei.

I was privileged to be in that room when Pei presented the design that would forever change the look, and the use, of one of the most famous buildings in the world. The distinguished group of French leaders he faced were startled, some were shocked; all were aware of the gravity of the decision that was about to be made. Whose view would prevail? That of Mitterrand, president of France, or Chirac, mayor of Paris?

The building in question was, of course, the *Musée de Louvre*. The challenge was twofold. First, to design a new entrance that would better accommodate the many thousands of visitors who flocked daily to the museum. Second, to repurpose and reorganize the museum's ancient warren of underground spaces. The answer that Pei proposed centered on a modernist pyramid made of glass that would dominate the *Cour Napoléon*, the museum's huge courtyard, and reveal the re-imagined underground spaces. The pyramid was daring, futuristic and grand, standing in stark contrast to its classical surroundings, yet complementing them as well.

We know the outcome of the meeting. President Mitterrand became convinced. In 1983, he commissioned Pei's design. Six years of construction and controversy followed, but when the new entrance pavilion opened to great acclaim in 1989, architectural history had been made.

I was in the room that day because I represented Pei's firm, I. M. Pei & Partners. We all knew that, among the many difficulties that the Louvre project faced, buy-in from the French people was key. The French president might approve, but would the citizenry; would the world? If Pei was confident, so was I, because I knew that Pei's persuasive ability was as strong as his architecture.

Pei officially retired in 1990. The glass pyramid was the crowning point of his illustrious career. In the year since the Louvre's new entrance had been in service, millions of visitors had streamed through it. Millions more came to the courtyard just to admire it. Placing routinely among the top three sights in Paris, the pyramid has assured that Paris remains a "must see" destination. Over the next thirty years, until the coronavirus pandemic upended everything, the Louvre became the most frequented museum in the world, with almost 10 million people coming in 2019 alone. And always, the pyramid has fulfilled its function as a doorway to the artwork inside the museum and has remained a work of art itself.

Pei died in 2019 at age 102. Coming to the United States from China at age 18, he had already formed his ambition. He received his first architecture degree in 1940, when he was 23; his second in 1946. During his long and award-winning career, he was responsible for one breakthrough piece of work after another all over the world. Let's take a look at his beginnings, and his accomplishments. And his one major setback in mid-career.

Ieoh Ming Pei was born on April 26, 1917, in Guangzhou, China, and raised in Hong Kong and Shanghai. His family was an ancient one, dating back to the Ming dynasty; its success and wealth had come from trade in traditional medicinal herbs. His father was a well-connected and high official with the Bank of China whose signature was on the country's currency. Young Pei came of age in a large, comfortable house with gardens and pavilions that gave him a deep appreciation of the natural world.

Although there were four other children in the family, Ieoh Ming was favored by his mother, known for her talent as a flutist. As a child, he alone accompanied her on Buddhist re-treats, and he was allowed to administer her pain medication when she developed cancer. She died when he was 13. The family splintered after that, with the five children being sent to live in various relatives' households and the father "living his own separate life," as Pei told a biographer years later. This kind of unfortunate early experience can either strengthen or weaken character; knowing the man as I did, I can say that it helped form his core values of excellence, resilience, sensitivity, and persistence.

Pei attended a rigorous Anglican secondary school in Shang-hai, a city known as the "Paris of the East," filled with beautiful gardens and colonial-era buildings. Early on, he formed the de-sire to go to college in the United States, partly because of what he learned by watching the American movies he enjoyed so much. As he told a biographer, "I decided that was the country for me."

Pei's movie-inspired decision may have been frivolous, but it was also grounded in career ambition. Many years later, he would tell *The New York Times* about his boyhood fascination with the construction of a hotel in Shanghai: "I couldn't resist looking into the hole. That's when I decided I wanted to build."

Relying on his research into American college catalogs, he enrolled—sight unseen—in the University of Pennsylvania to study architecture. Leaving home in 1935, he sailed to San Francisco and then took a train to Philadelphia. There he was quickly disenchanted. He was less proficient than his classmates at basic skills such as draftsmanship, and he realized that his interest was in modern architecture rather than the classical Beaux-Arts style that was prevalent in academia at that time. He decided to transfer to MIT and study engineering instead. A prescient professor intercepted him, though, and convinced him to return to the study of architecture. Even so, Pei continued to struggle between what he was being taught and what he increasingly saw as the future of architecture: the new so-called international style.

Engineering and architecture are distinct but complementary disciplines that are equally necessary to human endeavor. Engineering applies science and mathematics to solve problems pertaining to the design, building and use of engines, machines, and structures. Architecture is the art and the practice of designing and constructing buildings.

This struggle is a familiar one, isn't it? Having a vision for the future but needing to spend time laying a foundation. Knowing almost instinctively what your life should mean but needing to adhere to what the powers that be prescribe—for a while, at least.

I'm not being glib when I say that architects (and engineers) know how necessary it is to have strong foundations, but I imagine that Pei was very impatient during his time at MIT. Especially when he met the great modernist pioneer Le Corbusier and began to see how he could turn vision into reality. Pei was also greatly inspired by Frank Lloyd Wright and Ludwig Mies van der Rohe; later, by the Bauhaus movement. Even before he completed college, Pei knew where he wanted to go, where he *would* go. These early masters of architectural modernity were his models; his unique vision would extend modernity into its future.

Pei spent the decade of his twenties setting his course. He graduated from MIT at age 23, in 1940, winning the American Institute of Architects Gold Medal and belonging to Alpha Rho Chi, the fraternity of architects. He had already met his future wife, Eileen Loo, a Wellesley College student who had also emigrated from China. He considered returning to China or going to Europe, but wartime and post-war conditions dissuaded him; Pei would be 57 years old before he saw China again. In a whirlwind, within eight years, he married Eileen, held an MIT fellowship, worked for the National Defense Research Committee on bomb-related research that he never revealed, earned a master's degree in architecture from Harvard, and taught at Harvard. During that time, Eileen earned her own graduate degree from Harvard in landscape architecture. (Of their four children, two would be architects, one an urban planner and one a lawyer.)

In 1948, when Pei was 31, his career as a commercial architect began. He joined Webb and Knapp, the real estate firm owned by the heavyweight New York developer William Zeckendorf, as director of architecture. According to the *Boston Globe*, the flamboyant Zeckendorf had gone on a search for "the greatest unknown architect in the country" and found Pei.

Pei's work for Zeckendorf's firm encompassed a wide variety of projects, chief among them the Roosevelt Field Shopping Mall on Long Island, L'Enfant Plaza in Washington, D.C., and two in Denver, the Mile High Center and Courthouse Square. All these were notable because they involved not just single buildings, but a coordinated response to their urban environments.

In 1955, Pei (joined by two of his Harvard colleagues, Henry Cobb and Ulrich Franzen) formed his own semi-independent firm, with much work continuing to be commissioned by Webb and Knapp. Assignments included the Kips Bay development in New York City, the Royal Bank Plaza in Montreal, Society Hill in Philadelphia (including the Society Hill Towers), and the Cecil and Ida Green Building at MIT, home to the university's earth sciences department.

Pei was spending more and more of his time on project management, coordinating the myriad elements that go into such large commissions. He was supervising rather than designing. Less time was being spent on the actual creative aspects of architecture, on bringing his own ideas to fruition. In 1960, he and his colleagues officially broke away from Zeckendorf's firm. Continuing to be based in New York City but working throughout the world, Pei's firm employed as many as three hundred people and went through several name changes over the years. It evolved after his death into Pei Architects, the firm led today by his sons, Harvard-educated like their parents.

The years between 1960 and his Louvre triumph in 1989 were filled with projects large, small, consequential, and not. Commercial, corporate, and municipal buildings; academic buildings (including three more at his alma mater MIT, in addition to the Green Building); shopping malls, urban plazas, and housing developments; chapels and private homes; libraries (JFKs in Boston, the most prominent) and hotels; museums, symphony halls and other arts-related structures (the Rock and Roll Hall of Fame in Cleveland, for example); air traffic control towers and airline terminals. His style evolved from densely textured concrete facades (often with a waffle texture), to clean-lined geometric shapes, to almost experimental use of glass. In his hands, seemingly disparate building elements were juxtaposed with their natural surroundings in ways that made visual sense. Always, art and utility were married together.

Pei's work resulted in numerous awards for his individual projects, and for himself. On a personal level, the highest was the U.S. Presidential Medal of Freedom in 1992. For his professional accomplishments, he won the Gold Medal of the American Institute of Architects in 1979, the Pritzker Prize in 1983, the Japanese Praemium Imperiale in 1989, the RIBA Royal Gold Medal in 2010, and the UIA Gold Medal in 2014.

I referred earlier to the major setback in Pei's career. That was Hancock Place (originally planned as offices for the old-line John Hancock Insurance Company), designed by the Pei firm's Henry Cobb. I want to spend some time discussing this illustrative episode, which was "agonizing," according to the *Boston Globe*.

Groundbreaking for the sixty-story Hancock structure at Copley Square in Boston's Back Bay took place in 1968, and problems were immediately apparent. Excavation damaged the nearby historic Trinity Church, sewer lines, and other underground utilities. Sinkholes developed in Copley Square's soft ground. Worst of all, as construction progressed, the five-hundred-pound windows that formed the building's reflective-glass facade began falling out in the kind of winds that abound in Boston, especially in the winter. Initially, internal-external air pressure differentials were blamed; these also prevented the external doors from operating properly. As well, the building swayed in high winds.

According to *Architecture Week* in an article titled "When Bad Things Happen to Good Buildings," many theories and myths arose as explanations for the problems: Some thought the building swayed too much in the wind; that was an issue but not the cause of the popping windows. Others believed the rhomboid shape of the tower placed too much stress on the glass; that did cause some problems but was not the source of the trouble— the windows had been designed to handle much more stress than any of them were ever subjected to. Still others thought the trouble was the way the building was settling into its foundation. But no, explained the publication: "The problem actually lay in the insulating glass itself." The very feature that made the building so distinctive on the Boston skyline—its dramatic glass curtain—was its vulnerability.

Each pane of glass was actually a "sandwich"—two very thin panes with an insulating air space in between, the panes being held apart by lead-tape spacers copper-soldered to their edges. "The lead-tape seal insulating unit was the premier product of the time. It was expensive, but it performed very well with relatively small sheets of clear glass." The very large size of the Hancock's panes (fifty-five square feet each) was already problematic, and the reflective coatings and tints applied to the glass (the architect's vision for the building called for it to mirror Boston's skies) added substantial weight. This caused serious differential movement and increased stress along the glass-to-tape bond. Eventually, the bonds began to separate. The bond, however, was so strong in some areas that the tape ripped microscopically small pieces of glass from the window surfaces. These sites concentrated stress from wind loads, which ultimately proved catastrophic.

Hancock Place was supposed to have opened in 1971, but it was not until 1976 that all the problems were addressed. Every "sandwich" pane of glass—10,348 in all—was replaced with a high-strength monolithic pane. The swaying that the tower exhibited in windy conditions was addressed with "interior reinforcing to prevent walls and partitions from cracking," reported the *Boston Globe*. The cost of the building went from $75 million to $175 million. All these years later, Bostonians will tell of the "eye sores" (the sheets of plywood) hastily erected to cover the holes in the facade when the windows fell off; "Plywood Palace" became the Hancock's nickname. Providentially, there were no casualties from the falling glass and other problems, but lawsuits abounded.

Even though Hancock Place won the American Institute of Architects National Honor Award in 1977 and is one of the late twentieth century's most beautiful skyscrapers, the entire project was a major blow to the reputation of Pei's firm overall.

And to its finances. The *Boston Globe* said that the problems "hurt the firm badly," quoting Henry Cobb: "We were virtually blacklisted from corporate and development work for some years."

This episode was an excruciating personal embarrassment for I. M. Pei. He himself had not designed the building, nor specified the glass, but his name was synonymous with the firm's, and the firm's name was on the plans. As if to prove that he, at least, knew how to work with glass, he re-dedicated himself to the use of that material in his future designs. Never again would he be associated with such failure.

What lessons can come to us when we stumble and fall! We learn to correct mistakes, to accept responsibility, to prove ourselves again and again, as many times as necessary. We learn humility, perseverance, and how to do things in new and better ways. Putting one foot in front of the other, we move forward. I. M. Pei was not the first or the last to learn those lessons. I have had to, as well.

The Louvre pyramid, of course, was all about glass, the medium that had bedeviled the Hancock. The pyramid was all about using the transparency of glass to welcome visitors, to serve as a modern portal, to bring light into internal spaces. Equally as striking as the structure rising above the *Cour Napoléon* was its *inversée*, the complementary pyramidal structure that pierced the underground space of the museum's associated retail space beneath the courtyard. (Additionally, three smaller pyramids were located nearby on the courtyard.)

The Louvre project was successful not only because it was a superb piece of architecture but because of the way Pei won over the hearts and minds of the people, a process I was privileged to witness and that taught me a lot about public relations. It was not an easy process.

"The international response was swift, and it was brutal," wrote *Architect Magazine*. "Pei was publicly mocked." Summa-

rized *The New York Times*: "An architectural joke, an anachro-
nistic intrusion, a megalomaniacal folly." The CBC said that
the "futuristic" structure "was reviled" by many French. A French
newspaper described Pei's pyramids as "an annex to Disney-
land" while an environmental group said they "belonged in a
desert." Many questioned why Egyptian tombs were being
built in Paris (ignoring the fact of Egyptian artifacts in the
Louvre's collections).

Pei quickly found himself in the center of an international
controversy, accused of defacing one of the world's great land-
marks. He argued that his glass pyramid was merely an updated
version of a traditional form, and that his redesigned courtyard
had been influenced by the geometric work of the French landscape architect Le Nôtre. It was rigorously rational, in other
words, and in that sense classically French.

Pei had already completed a self-directed four-month education process, immersing himself in the Louvre itself and French
history and culture, so he had the ammunition at hand to deflect popular criticism. He also had the quick wit to parry such
criticism. When he was told, "You're American, so you don't
respect tradition," he would reply: "But I'm also Chinese and
we respect tradition."

During construction, Pei was omnipresent at the site. He
wanted to track progress, of course, but he also wanted to take
the pulse of onlookers, whose curiosity and concern ran high.
Here is what he said in a PBS documentary: "I would say the
first year was really hell. I couldn't walk the streets of Paris
without people looking at me and saying, 'What are you doing
here? What are you doing to us? What are you doing to our
great Louvre?'"

One answer to those man-on-the-street questions might
have been that Pei was helping preserve the massive but increasingly fragile Louvre, parts of which date to the twelfth
century. The entrance pavilion would help spread out the
weight of the "human" load of so many visitors. The under-

ground work would address necessary infrastructure issues. Perhaps Pei could have added "historical preservation expert" to his résumé.

The glass pyramid was no flash-in-the-pan. In 2017, two years before Pei's death, the AIA awarded the Louvre project its Twenty-Five Year Award, given annually to a building "that has stood the test of time by embodying architectural excellence for 25 to 35 years."

"At one level, my goal is simply to give people pleasure in being in a space and walking around it. But I also think architecture can reach a level where it influences people to want to do something more with their lives. That is the challenge I find most interesting"—I. M. Pei said that specifically about the Louvre accomplishment.

But I think it is a fitting coda for the entire body of work that Pei represented, and for the man himself. Not only did he inspire people "to do something more" in the abstract sense, he provided the material means as well. He used his $100,000 Pritzker Prize money to fund an ongoing program for Chinese architects to study in the United States—and then return to China to practice.

16

AKIO MORITA
(Japan, United States)

For the background and insights they so generously imparted to me about Mr. Morita, I am grateful to Mr. Kanji Yamanouchi, ambassador and consul general of Japan in New York; Mr. Daisuke Sakuraba, consul in New York; and Ms. Hiroko Onoyama, retired vice president of Sony Corporation of America and assistant to Mr. Morita.

EXPECTATIONS ARE A HEAVY WEIGHT for anyone to bear, especially a young person. Knowing that parents, teachers, society want you to do or be something that you don't want to do or be can be frustrating and deadening. Even just feeling instinctively that this might be happening can be paralyzing. If these expectations are emerging from family history or long tradition, guilt at causing disappointment can be the result.

Now imagine that you are a young person grappling with such personal issues at a time when larger issues are overwhelming the world—the coronavirus pandemic, for example. Or when your country has just been defeated—much of it destroyed—in a war in which you served. What is your future; what is your country's future?

In simplistic terms, this challenge faced Akio Morita in August 1945, when he was 24 years old. He had delayed committing to follow in his ancestors' footsteps, to enter his family's centuries-old sake-brewing business. Instead, he had enrolled in a combined university-military program during World War II. Now, Hiroshima and Nagasaki lay in ruins from two atomic bombs dropped by the American forces, and Japan had surrendered to the Allies. What now?

Some forty years later, in his autobiography *Made in Japan*, Morita recalled that he was reeling from the realization that there would be dramatic changes in store not just for him, but for Japan. He had been thinking for a long time about the future, and he concluded that his homeland would need all the talent it could summon up. "I don't mind saying that even then, as a young man, I felt that somehow I had a role to play," he wrote. "I didn't know how big a role it would turn out to be."

Sake-making, no matter how important to his family's history and identity, would not be in Akio Morita's future. In general terms, his role would be "to help bring Japan and the United States and other Western nations closer together," he wrote. Specifically, the next year he and Masaru Ibuka founded the company that became the world-famous consumer electronics firm Sony.

When Akio Morita was born on January 26, 1921, he was the first son in the fifteenth generation of his very wealthy and influential family, representing four hundred years of producing sake as well as essential Japanese staples such as soy sauce and miso paste. The weight of expectations was on the infant from his very first day, and Akio grew up "carrying the first son's burden." His life was bound up in tradition, just as his father's had been. His father was also a first son who had to abandon his studies in order to rescue the family firm years earlier when it almost faced bankruptcy. Akio's father had succeeded, and he did not want the Morita family or firm to face such dire circumstances again. Akio represented the future.

"I was made aware of my family tradition and my ancestors from early childhood," Morita wrote. His father was determined that his first born learn the family business and step into the influential role in Japan that the Morita family had held for so long. There was little fun involved. *Work* was involved, and constant reminders of his destiny. "As a young boy in middle school, my holidays were consumed by business, business, business," he later said.

Actually, it started younger than that. About the age of 10 he was taken to the company office at the sake brewery and shown how the business was run. He sat in at his father's side in business meetings that to such a youngster naturally seemed long and boring. And always he was told, he said, "You are the eldest son in the family. Remember that." He was never allowed to forget that he would be his father's successor, both as the head of the family company and as the head of the household.

Along with meetings and stock-checking and sake-tasting, his father Kyuzaemon imparted lessons to his son that would transcend the sake business. The wisdom of these life lessons would become part of the Sony ethos: "I was taught how to talk to people who work for you. I was cautioned time and again as a young man, 'Don't think that because you are at the top you can boss others around.'" Be very clear on what you have decided to do and what you ask others to do, he was told, and take full responsibility for your decisions.

He was also taught that scolding employees and looking for scapegoats were useless. This highly useful lesson made him realize the value of motivating others to accomplish things that would be to everyone's advantage. Everybody wants to succeed.

As a boy, Akio learned to be patient, understanding, unselfish, and kind. He listened to others and paid attention to their needs. He valued collecting differing opinions from others, while at the same time forming his own views. These were traits that he became known for at Sony, along with his great curiosity. He would meet with anyone who wanted to see him, even if just for a minute, because of what he might learn.

For his development, he credited not only his father's example as a business leader, but also his family's Buddhist religion. And he credited his mother, Shuko, "a clever woman of great patience; a quiet, artistic, and gentle woman."

Shuko, the seventh daughter of her parents, had also been born into a family with a long and distinguished history; in her case, in banking. She possessed an unusual combination of qualities for any woman at the time of Akio's childhood in the 1920s, certainly for a Japanese woman of her class. She balanced tradition with being progressive and open to new ideas. Known as a quiet and gentle woman, she was also "very assertive" and held "firm opinions," remembered Akio, especially about the value of education for her children. Most importantly, from the point of view of her first son, who felt the burden of family expectations, she was a very understanding and supportive mother: "I felt she understood everything, and she was easy to talk to. Certainly, easier than my father, whose life was dominated by the business . . . so I went to her more often than to my father for advice and help."

As Akio grew into his teenage years, he tried to balance his mother's support with what he knew his father wanted—and with what he himself was more and more drawn to: "electronic tinkering," as he called it. He was dedicated and very curious about many things, though not necessarily his schoolwork. He had a workbench at home where he disassembled and then reassembled his "toys"—radios, phonographs, recorders, and so forth—in order to understand their mechanisms and functions. He bought books and subscribed to magazines about electronics. These activities distracted him from his studies so much that he, though a smart child, was always seated up front under the eye of the teacher with the slow learners. He did well at math, physics, and geometry, but not in geography, history, or Japanese. In an understatement, Akio admitted a "lack of interest in conventional studies," with the expected result: "When it would get really bad, my parents would scold me and order me to put away my electronic toys. I would obey until my grades began to look a little better, and then I would go back to the things I liked best."

Akio's love of "toys" extended into his adulthood. In the library and education center located in Tokoname City, Aichi Prefecture, on the premises of the Morita family's historic home, a special exhibit showcases his treasures. These include the miniature street organ, the nickelodeon, and the antique player piano that were his favorites. Wrote his wife Yoshiko: "My husband, who could not see an old or unusual sound-producing machine without immediately wanting to own it, would say, 'Sorry, I went and bought another one. Where are you going to put it?' We often had such conversations in those days." Subject to pandemic-related restrictions, the facility is open to the public; check akiomorita.com for information. The entire library can be accessed any time via akiomorita.net and is well worth a virtual visit.

Let's circle back to the kind of family in which Akio Morita grew up; it was an uncommon one, and not only because of its long-standing wealth and influence.

On one level, the family was very traditional and conservative; on another, it was unusually modern. Kyuzaemon was a generous man who indulged his family and was attentive to his four children. He liked to take them fishing, and they played tennis on their own court. He was always "interested in new, imported technologies and foreign products." In traditional kimono attire at home, he wore Western attire to work. Shuko loved Western classical music and owned a "tinny-sounding Victrola," later replaced by a better model, also a Victor. The sounds of Ravel, Mozart, Bach, and Beethoven flowed through the house. The Morita family owned Ford Model T and Model A automobiles, as well as Westinghouse and GE appliances. Everyone enjoyed American movies.

The household itself was quite large, with as many as twenty people at any given time. Living there were parents, grandparents, children, and a widowed aunt. An uncle, having spent four years studying art in France, returned bringing "a personal account of the outside world to us, and we were all intrigued." Additionally, there were always several stay-in-home students (boarders, essentially) from other families, as well as housekeepers and other helpers. Shuko managed all this with smooth assurance.

Here is a very early indication of how Akio's parents would balance tradition with modernity—deciding what to name him at birth. In the Morita family for most of its history, first sons were named either Tsunesuke or Hikotaro; when they assumed their role as head of the family (and the business), that name would be changed to Kyuzaemon. Upon retirement, another name would be taken because "Kyuzaemon" would be passed on to the new head. When Shuko and Kyuzaemon's first son was born, it was his turn to be named Tsunesuke, but his parents thought it was too old-fashioned and consulted a venerable Japanese scholar for advice. Akio was the result.

The characters for "Akio" and "Morita" sum up to "prosperous rice field," auspicious for someone destined for the sake (which is made from rice) business. Because Akio never took over the family business, but struck out on his own, he never officially became "Kyuzaemon," though he would often use the initials "AKM" as his monogram.

As the time for secondary school leading to college approached, Akio made a decision that presaged some of the characteristics he would show as a business leader—independence, determination, diligence, and preparation. He told his parents and teachers that he wanted to specialize in science. He had good grades in that field (mathematics too), but he faced a very competitive situation, and a dilemma. His overall grades were poor, and he faced some tough examinations on subjects that he had neglected in order to get into a university with a good science department. "I knew it, but I was determined," he later wrote. "And so, I became a *ronin*."

A *ronin* is an ancient word for someone who has, so to speak, gotten off-track and must find his own way. So Akio devoted himself to a year of study with tutors to help him make up his academic shortcomings: "For one year I buckled down and studied harder than I had ever studied. I didn't do anything else that whole year but study. And I made it."

Greater problems lay in wait for Akio than his grades. Simmering societal unrest began to boil over, with assassinations aimed at the privileged classes in 1932, an attempted government insurrection by ultranationalist fascists in 1936, and the ongoing buildup of hostilities against the Soviet Union and China.

The ultranationalist revolt had failed, but the attempt aroused the sympathy of many people, and upper-class politicians and businessmen were intimidated. Worse, the nation was in poor economic condition. "Whenever my father and his friends would get together," Akio said, "they would talk of the dangers ahead."

Worldwide war was approaching and then became a reality. Germany invaded Poland in September 1939. The attack on Pearl Harbor in December 1941—which was as shocking to most Japanese as it was to the rest of the world—brought the United States into World War II. "Everyone in our house was stunned by this news, and I remember thinking that this was a dangerous thing . . . that a mistake had been made."

Even as life changed, life went on. In the Japanese educational structure, secondary school encompassed what in the United States would be considered high school plus the first two years of college. In 1942, when Akio graduated from secondary school—focused not only on science, but specifically on physics ("I wanted to know why things worked")—he was 21. Obviously, the reality of military service loomed for Akio, but not yet. He was on his way to two more years at the relatively new Osaka Imperial University, already a groundbreaking center for serious physics researchers and students. And he was continuing to flout—respectfully, no doubt—his father's expectation that he would go into business economics. Even when it was clear that Akio was set on science for his college career, his father thought he would study agricultural chemistry, which would at least be relevant to the brewing industry. He never tried to change his son's mind, "but I am sure he still expected me to assume my role in the family when the time came. He believed that physics would eventually be only a hobby for me."

At university, Akio took every opportunity possible to work in a favorite professor's laboratory, which was now doing naval research. It was through this work that he was introduced to atomic energy. At the time, the idea of an atomic weapon seemed remote. There were two cyclotrons in Japan, but progress toward creating an atomic reaction was progressing very slowly, and of course no one in Japan—or Germany—had any inkling about the United States' Manhattan Project.

As a student during wartime, Akio faced several options—including just waiting to be drafted—but by the time he graduated from Osaka in 1944, he had no choice: "We physics students were put under direct military control like everyone else in the country; I was assigned to the Office of Aviation Technology at Yokosuka in early 1945." And so it was that Akio was at his station in Yokosuka in August 1945 when the atomic bombs were dropped on Hiroshima and Nagasaki, and when Japan surrendered, and the war ended. All expectations were off the table.

Even though "the war with the United States was a tragedy," wrote Morita, "the new period of peace was strange." Japan was a devastated country, although the Morita family lost very little in the material sense; they suffered no personal casualties, and the household and business facilities were relatively unscathed. Life changed again and continued to go on.

The most consequential changes centered on the Japanese people's expectations for themselves and their society. A spirit of renewal, rebirth, and freedom began to emerge from tragedy. Looking forward to the future, even if it was unknown, was more important than looking back constantly to the traditions of the past. It was time to do things in a new way.

That shift became evident in the Morita family. His father was still healthy and robust and in charge of the business, so there wasn't any pressing need for Akio, now 24, at the office. Everybody agreed there would be plenty of time for him to take charge later. It must have been a relief for Morita to have the long-held family expectations relaxed and to have the opportunity to move toward his own goals. He lost no time.

During his relatively short military service, Morita had worked with a brilliant electronics engineer, Masaru Ibuka. Senior to Morita by thirteen years, Ibuka had already established his own company; he would become Morita's "very close friend, colleague, partner." By the end of 1945, the two men were back in touch. In 1946, they founded the predecessor of what, a dozen years of false starts and smart moves later, would be listed on the Tokyo Stock Exchange as the Sony Corporation. The Sony Corporation of America would be formed in 1960. Two years later, it became the first Japanese company to list on the New York Stock Exchange. It was also the first Japanese company to build a factory in the United States.

What happened to the expectations that Akio would become the next Kyuzaemon? Something earth-shattering. Something astonishing. Something almost unheard of. Put simply, his father gave his blessing to his first son's venture with Masaru Ibuka.

How had this acceptance come about? As a father myself, I think that the elder Morita, who knew his son well and watched his development closely, finally took to heart the young man's ambitions for himself. Kyuzaemon Morita also had the breadth and depth of character to recognize that, just as Japanese society was in the midst of change, his family also needed to adapt to new ways. As difficult as it was, the elder Morita said to his son, "You are going to do what you like best."

In addition to paternal moral support, Kyuzaemon Morita also offered practical support—loans that were repaid with stock awards, eventually making him a major shareholder.

Eventually, the second son, Kazuaki, assumed what would have been Akio's role. In the fullness of time, Akio's own first son, Hideo, became head of the family business, which continues to this day; his second son, Masao, worked for Sony, as did his brother Masaaki. His sister Kikuko married his childhood friend Kazuo Iwama, who joined the Ibuka/Morita venture in its early days and later became a Sony president.

Akio Morita was 25 years old when he partnered with Masaru Ibuka to fulfill what he knew was his destiny: "to help bring Japan and the United States and other Western nations closer together." Sony became a worldwide company focused on transforming visionary ideas into desirable products that people both needed and wanted. Freed of burdensome family expectations, Morita willingly shouldered new ones of his own choice: Expectations from employees, colleagues, customers, shareholders, and others involved in the success of Sony. Expectations from the family that he, his wife Yoshiko, and their three children would form.

How did the Sony name come about? Ikuba and Morita wanted something easy to pronounce in any language, easy to grasp and recognize and that did not carry a preordained meaning. They and their products would infuse it with meaning. They wanted a name that would become a symbol. "Sony" was related to the Latin words *sonitus* or *sonus* (meaning sound) and to the American slang expression "sonny boy" (someone who is young and favored). Thus, Ikuba and Morita were young guys, on their way up, interested in sound.

Akio Morita retired in 1994 and died on October 3, 1999, at age 78. His obituary in *The New York Times* extolled him as the man who "personified Japan's rise from postwar rubble to industrial riches and became the unofficial ambassador of its business community to the world."

Sony became one of the world's most innovative companies, famous for products like transistor radios, videocassette recorders, the Walkman, and the compact disc.

To the day of his death, he was Japan's most famous business executive, and the only one many Americans could name or recognize in a photograph. *Time* magazine recently selected him as one of twenty "most influential business geniuses" of the twentieth century, the only non-American on the list.

Akio Morita, noted for his highly refined business acumen, especially in marketing, also possessed a great deal of down-to-earth wisdom. This he accumulated through experience. His teachings were published as essays in Sony's corporate magazine and elsewhere; they are collected on the website akiomorita.net under "The Sayings of Akio Morita—A Textbook for the Heart." I'll give just one example. From which of his personal experiences do you think this came?

What on earth does educational background mean? Does it carry any value? For people working in the cutthroat world of business, you have to fight using all of your abilities, and however I look at it, I can't see the value of judging people on the place they studied before joining the company. What a person studied and where they studied is just an asset, and it is how that person uses that asset and what contribution they make to society that decides the value of that person. No matter how much demand there may be in business for specialist learning found in universities, in reality, it is a fact that the smartest kid in school will not necessarily become the most gifted person in society.

17

MARIA TALLCHIEF

(United States)

MARIA TALLCHIEF WAS THE FIRST Native American prima ballerina—in the sense that she was born in the United States—and
the first Native American prima ballerina—because she was a
daughter of the Osage Nation.

On November 27, 1949, the opening night of the premier of
The Firebird for the New York City Ballet, she danced the title
role in a way that established her greatness and assured that her
brilliance would never be forgotten. She was 24 years old and
had been dancing professionally for seven years and on her career path for twenty-one. From when she was a very little girl,
she had known—or she so absorbed her mother's ambitions
that they became hers—that she would be a star.

According to Paul Lang's account of Tallchief's debut in *The
Firebird*, in the biography *Maria Tallchief: Native American Ballerina,* from the moment she made her first leap onto the stage,
"The New York City Center audience was spellbound. This
exotic, passionate creature seemed to have flown into the spotlight from another world." Lang went on to describe how her
final entrance in the ballet "was greeted with wild applause."
And when the curtain fell, "The audience rose to its feet and
cheered so loudly, according to one spectator, 'it was as if we
were in a football stadium instead of a theater.'"

Tallchief's performance that night, in addition to what it

meant in terms of personal achievement, assured that the one-year-old New York City Ballet—founded to showcase American dancers, a new concept in the Russian- and European-centered world of ballet—would develop into the premier institution it remains today.

Tallchief revolutionized American ballet, not just demographically, but through her immense physical talents, her strength, her precision, her devotion to excellence. Her influence never faded. It can almost be said that she invented American ballet, her work and persona were so distinct; she certainly came to personify it. As the poet Yeats asked, in a different time and another context: "How can we know the dancer from the dance?"

It is a challenge to be an individual, to maintain your uniqueness as you seek—and hope—to find your place in the world. But it's also a challenge to be viewed as a representative of a larger group, to know that your actions reflect on other people and may affect their ability to find their place. Tallchief faced both, always on the public stage.

Tallchief's path was set from age 3, when her precocity in both music and dance was noticed and nurtured. Years of training in both disciplines followed. Her career as a ballerina began when she was 17 and spanned the years 1942–1966. Retiring from performing at age 41, she continued her influence as director of ballet for the Lyric Opera of Chicago and founder and co-artistic director of the Chicago City Ballet and School. Awards and accolades flowed her way throughout her life; there was not a detractor to be found. Receiving a Kennedy Center Honor in 1996, Tallchief remarked on what she wanted that particular honor to represent: "I hope it will set a precedent for young American ballerinas. You don't have to be from Russia." (It was a happy event that, in 1960, she had been the first American to dance at the Bolshoi Theater in Moscow.)

Most known for her association with the New York City Ballet, she began her career with the Ballet Russe de Monte-Carlo and also appeared with the Paris Opera Ballet, the American Ballet Theatre, the Chicago Opera Ballet, the San Francisco Ballet, the Royal Danish Ballet, and the Hamburg Ballet.

When she died in 2013, age 88, she was compared to two of the century's greatest ballerinas by the choreographer Jacques d'Amboise, who was a lowly corps dancer when she starred in *The Firebird.* D'Amboise said, "When you thought of the Russian ballet, it was [Galina] Ulanova of the Soviet Union. With English ballet, it was [Dame Margot] Fonteyn. For American ballet, it was Tallchief. She was grand in the grandest way."

Born in Fairfax, Oklahoma, on January 24, 1925, Elizabeth ("Betty") Marie Tall Chief was the second of three children of Ruth Porter Tall Chief and Alexander Tall Chief. Ruth was of Irish-Scottish-German descent and Alexander was full-blooded Osage. His three older children from a previous marriage, also to a woman of European descent, lived nearby with their grandmother Eliza Bigheart Tall Chief. All in all, Betty's family was the most prominent in Fairfax.

In 1871, the ages-old Osage Nation was forced by the United States government to consolidate into what became the state of Oklahoma in 1907. The land was obviously poor, not suited for hunting and farming, but unbeknownst to the government, vast stores of oil and gas lay underground. Once extraction began, income from "mineral rights" was paid to each Osage in regular allotments.

As the Depression opened and deepened, the oil-rich Osage Nation did not suffer as keenly as did most of America. Years earlier, "oil was discovered on Osage land, and overnight the tribe became rich," wrote Maria Tallchief in her 1997 autobiography. She continued, "As a young girl growing up on the Osage reservation . . . I felt my father owned the town." And for good reason—he owned the town's pool hall and its movie theater, and the family lived in a ten-room house that stood on a hill overlooking the reservation.

There was a price to be paid, however, in the Tall Chief family. Speaking of her father, Maria said, "Like many in the wealthy Osage tribe, Daddy had never worked a day in his life. He was modern-day Osage in another respect. He drank. His drinking ran in cycles, mostly when the oil royalties check arrived."

Ruth, who knew great deprivation in her childhood, wanted only the best for her children, especially her artistically talented daughters, Betty Marie and Marjorie. Within the limitations of their small town, Ruth made sure that classical music and dance lessons were part of the girls' childhoods. Thinking back to how she was at that young age, Tallchief wrote, "I simply did what she asked. I wanted to please."

The girls' older brother, Jerry, was incapacitated by a nutritional deficiency at birth and a serious accident at age 4. He required much parental attention growing up, leading Betty Marie to wonder if "Mother's disappointment in Jerry is what caused her to turn her attention to Marjorie and me, making it so important to her that we succeed."

As much as Ruth focused on classical arts, the influence of the family's Native American heritage was transmitted in equal measure by Eliza Bigheart, "a majestic figure," as Betty Marie recalled. Surreptitiously, the girls' grandmother took them to powwows and other tribal ceremonies; such events had been banned by government edicts aimed at destroying traditional customs. Betty Marie grew up knowing Chopin as well as she knew the rattling of gourds and the tinkling of bells, doing pliés and turnouts as naturally as shuffling side to side in the steps typical of Osage women dancers.

Such a lot for a young girl to absorb! As a parent, I understand Ruth. As the son of parents who had high standards for their children, I also understand Betty Marie. It must have been tough—pleasing her mother, seeing the effects of her father's drinking, navigating life with a special-needs sibling, balancing diverse cultures within the family structure, knowing that much was expected of her. Not all of us handle these realities grace-fully or successfully. Maria Tallchief did, then and in the rest of her life.

In 1933, when Betty Marie was eight and Marjorie six, the family moved to California, to find more opportunities for the girls. As Betty Marie wrote: "My mother grew increasingly dis-satisfied with our life in Fairfax. To her it was a place where people wasted their lives . . . where her daughters remained in small-town music and ballet lessons that never would amount to much."

First in Los Angeles and then in Beverly Hills, Ruth found what she wanted for her daughters: esteemed teachers who could mold the girls into stars. Yet there was still a price to be paid, as any child whose parents have moved the family to a new community can attest. It's hard to be new. Wrote Tallchief: "I was made to feel different." It started at school, with her very name: "Some of the students made fun of my last name, pretending they didn't understand if it was Tall or Chief. Eventually, I turned the spelling of my last name into one word."

Marjorie followed suit with the new spelling; eventually, her parents did too. Even so, the girls' Native American heritage continued to be misunderstood and mocked: "A few [students] made war whoops whenever they saw me," Maria Tallchief later wrote, "and asked why I didn't wear feathers or if my fa-ther took scalps." A man Ruth had met through the dance school convinced her that Betty Marie and Marjorie should work up a Native American dance. Ruth liked the idea and soon the girls were performing at venues like county fairs and fraternal lodge benefits. Betty Marie did not share in her mother's enthusiasm: "The routine we performed made us both self-conscious. It wasn't remotely authentic. Traditionally, women didn't dance in Indian tribal ceremonies."

When Betty Marie was 12 and Marjorie almost 11, Ruth enrolled them in the studio that the famed Russian ballerina (and sister to the even more famed Nijinsky) Bronislava Nijinska, always called Madame, had established in Beverly Hills. Ballet did not yet have its own American identity; the classic Russian style prevailed and a watershed event for the girls was seeing the stars from the Ballet Russe de Monte-Carlo, on tour in Los Angeles, arrive at the studio to pay their respects to Madame. Thriving under Madame's rigor and becoming her protégé, Betty Marie was torn, because Ruth was pushing her toward a career as a concert pianist. Betty Marie's dilemma was evident at a recital during her early teens, when she—with excellence—both played Bach and Mozart in the first half and danced in the second.

Ballet prevailed. Betty Marie's musicality was a factor in her success as a dancer, but her future was evident. The appropriate introductions were made for Madame's protégé, who by this time had come to the attention of other well-known artists and teachers. At age 17, having just graduated from high school and done little other than dance, Betty Marie was on her way—to New York and her own place with the Ballet Russe de Monte-Carlo and to her defining career. (Marjorie followed a few years later; she would enjoy her own very successful ballet career.)

Betty Marie Tall Chief's name continued its evolution to "Maria Tallchief." We've already seen how, as a child, she modified her family name to lessen the opportunity for ethnic ridicule. But, rejecting a common practice among American dancers, she refused to "Russianize" her name; she would never be "Tallchieva." Apparently, her given name was also problematic; unsophisticated, perhaps too redolent of her "Okie" roots? She became "Maria" in 1942 on the advice of Agnes de Mille, the legendary choreographer.

At the time, de Mille was rehearsing the groundbreaking and quintessentially American ballet, *Rodeo*, with music by Aaron Copland. Betty Marie was a mere member of the ensemble, certainly not a soloist. One afternoon, as she wrote in her autobiography, "Miss de Mille found me in the studio . . . [and said], 'I have some advice. There are so many Bettys and Elizabeths in ballet. If I were you, I'd think about changing my name. Why don't you use your middle name alone and call yourself Maria?'"

No career is easy, just as no true accomplishment is; we all know that. But even as it exudes such glamour, ballet has to be one of the least glamorous careers. The grace and beauty projected onstage are the product of tough athletic training and iron discipline. Competition is fierce, jealousy is rampant, and one false move—literally, a slip onstage, a seemingly minor injury—can end a career, especially in its beginning stages. Manipulation of young dancers is common because of the inherent power imbalance in the hierarchical structure of any troupe or company. Maria Tallchief faced all this, and more, in her seven years with the Ballet Russe de Monte-Carlo.

In 1944, the heralded dancer and choreographer George Balanchine joined the Ballet Russe. He had defected from Russia two decades earlier, at age 20, presaging dancer/choreographer Rudolf Nureyev's action in defecting from the Soviet Union in the early 1960s. He was a star in the world where Tallchief's ambition was taking her. (I'm thinking of the irony of her statement some forty years later, at the Kennedy Center: "You don't have to be from Russia.")

Nureyev was associated with many of the great international and American ballet companies, but never with the New York City Ballet. For a New York City Opera production in 1979, near the end of his life, Balanchine choreographed a ballet specifically for Nureyev; the only one, as it was his view that Nureyev could choreograph his own work for himself. Nureyev chose Tallchief as his partner in his American debut in 1962; they were close friends until his death in 1993. Interestingly, Tallchief's partner in her 1960 appearance at the Bolshoi Theater was Erik Bruhn, the young Danish phenom who became world famous in his own right and as Nureyev's romantic partner.

Soon, Tallchief became Balanchine's muse. A muse is not a role that involves an audition; rather, it is an alchemical relationship—as with directors and actors, or artists and models, choreographers need dancers to fulfill their visions, dancers need choreographers to provide their material. *The New York Times* acknowledged as much, extolling Tallchief in its obituary as "a dazzling ballerina and muse for Balanchine." But there are two sides to any coin. *The Washington Post* wrote in its obituary of Tallchief, "Balanchine . . . was known to fixate on one woman, making her his artistic obsession and romantic partner, only to eventually abandon her when a new talent came along."

Soon the professional partnership became personal, and in 1946, they married. The questions have to be asked. Was Tallchief a pawn of Balanchine? Did she go from her mother's influence to his? Did he see her as a vessel for his long-held ambition, as a tool to assure his own greatness? Did he become a vessel or a tool for her? On both the professional and personal levels, the power imbalance was obvious. She was a novice young dancer only four years into her career; he was already a seasoned and dominant figure. She was 21 when they married; he was 40 and already thrice married. I can't answer those questions. Is it enough that the work he/she did together, spoke for itself? Or that Tallchief viewed her time with Balanchine as "the most significant artistic event of her life"? She said later: "I never really understood, until Balanchine, what ballet was all about."

In 1947, along with arts patron Lincoln Kirstein, Balanchine formed the Ballet Society, which became the New York City Ballet in 1948. In 1949, Tallchief's contract with the Ballet Russe having expired, he choreographed *The Firebird* specifically for her. Their combined accomplishment with that work assured the success of the new ballet company and changed not only American, but all ballet permanently.

The Firebird, with a score by Igor Stravinsky, dates to 1910 and was his breakthrough work. It has been staged, restaged, choreographed, and re-choreographed many, many times and remains influential not only as an orchestral and dance work, but in popular culture. The Balanchine/Tallchief version, which included scenery and costumes by Marc Chagall, remained in the New York City Ballet's repertory until 1965.

Their personal union lasted until 1951, their professional one until the mid-1960s, when Tallchief retired as a dancer; her career had seemed to rise up in a straight line with nary a detour. Judge for yourself: Videos of Maria Tallchief's work are readily available online. Of all her roles, perhaps the ones Balanchine created for her were the most striking, according to the *New York Times*; in addition to *The Firebird*, she danced the Swan Queen in his version of *Swan Lake*, the Sugar Plum Fairy in his version of *The Nutcracker*, Eurydice in *Orpheus*, and principal roles in plotless works like *Sylvia Pas de Deux*, *Allegro Brillante*, *Pas de Dix*, and *Scotch Symphony*.

After the annulment of her marriage to Balanchine in 1951, Tallchief had a brief second marriage. In 1956, she married Henry Paschen, who died in 2004; they had one child, the poet Elise Paschen.

Among the many accolades given to Maria Tallchief, I am most moved by the mural entitled "Flight of Spirit" in the Oklahoma State Capitol. Painted in classical style by Mike Larsen, a noted Oklahoma artist of Chickasaw heritage, the mural pays tribute to five world-famous Native American ballerinas hailing from the state. Known as "the five moons," these women— Yvonne Chouteau, Rosella Hightower, Moscelyne Larkin, Maria Tallchief, and Marjorie Tallchief—gathered at the mural's dedication in 1991. All of the same generation, all born in the 1920s, they had never been all together at the same time. Even so, I think of them now as a virtual—in today's sense of the word—company of dancers. Maria was the prima, to be sure, but every soloist needs a supporting cast.

18

MAYA ANGELOU
(United States)

SOME MAY SAY THAT MY ABILITY to understand, appreciate, and tell the story of Maya Angelou, a Black woman, is limited by my identity as an American White man. Race relations is a fraught, front-and-center issue in our society. Racial injustice is a reality, as we continue to struggle with historical and systemic racism and its many manifestations. Just as I did earlier in this book with the story of Branch Rickey and Jackie Robinson, I want to acknowledge that maybe it's possible that I don't understand enough of Maya Angelou's story to do it justice. But I need and want to try, just as I did with Rickey and Robinson, because we all have a part to play in making things better.

Was Maya Angelou successful?

If you look at her accomplishments, her bestselling books, her awards and honors, her fame, her admirers, her legacy, her wealth—yes. If you look at her setbacks, her tragedies, her mistakes, her losses—maybe not. But those judgments represent how *you* look at her. How did she look at *herself*? Did Maya Angelou believe she was successful?

Judging by her own words, I would say, "Yes, she did." She defined success on her own terms, as she did everything else. Here is the simple truth she expressed so well: "Success is loving life and daring to live it."

For a seemingly simple word, "success" carries a lot of bag-gage. Too often, people can feel that if they are not regarded by others as influential, renowned, famous, accomplished, stars, and so forth, they are not "successful." If they don't measure up to someone else's standards, they have failed. Too often, we forget that, just as every person is unique, every person's path through life is unique. The people profiled in this book demon-strate that a dancer's path will be different from a scientist's, an athlete's from a novelist's, a general's from a mogul's. Paths will also be different because of race, nationality, gender, education, family, financial position, and many other factors.

Maya Angelou's path twisted through a very difficult early life, a troubled adolescence, a tough young adulthood. She sur-vived those times by putting one foot in front of the other, al-ways moving forward, even when the path was dark and rocky. She was nearly 30 before the path became smoother and brighter. Yet even as she grew into the woman that the world came to know and admire, challenges abounded. All along, it was clear that she never shirked away from life; she loved it and she lived it with daring. She was a success.

As she grew, she created her own unique Black woman's voice and spoke with it far and wide. She accepted and em-braced her life, even the ugly and hurtful parts. She told the stories of her life in ways no one else could and became a monument to personal truth-telling. Every one of us can learn from her bravery, candor, and artistry. I know that I have.

A woman of color. A woman of words—poems, autobiogra-phies, essays, plays, scripts, cookbooks, and books for children. A woman of performances—song and dance and theater and film and spoken-word recitation. A woman of civil rights and political activism in the United States and abroad. A woman with only a high school degree who held a lifetime university professorship and fifty honorary degrees. A woman who had been abused and raped and silenced as a child, who became a mother as a teenager, who did anything she could—sex worker, streetcar operator, line cook—to support herself and her son. A woman with brilliant talent and purpose who was comfortable everywhere, from the most modest surroundings to the grandest of the world's stages. All this, and more, was Maya Angelou.

Of Dr. Angelou's nearly forty published and produced works, the one most people know best is the autobiography *I Know Why the Caged Bird Sings*, published in 1969. It was the first nonfiction bestseller by a Black woman and tells of her life until age 18 or so. Its longevity can be seen in the history of its awards, stretching from the American Library Association's Coretta Scott King Book Award in 1971 to the National Book Foundation's Literarian Award in 2013. It was called "scathing and sardonic . . . joyous and painful . . . mysterious and memorable."

The book's title is an homage to the poem "Sympathy" by Paul Lawrence Dunbar (1872–1906), one of the first prominent Black writers. The final stanza reads:

I know why the caged bird sings, ah me,
When his wing is bruised and his bosom sore,—
When he beats his bars and he would be free;
It is not a carol of joy or glee,
But a prayer that he sends from his heart's deep core,
But a plea, that upward to Heaven he flings—
I know why the caged bird sings!

I Know Why the Caged Bird Sings came about after the 1968 assassination of Martin Luther King Jr. In a meeting with the writer James Baldwin and the cartoonist Jules Feiffer, Angelou was inspired to write about the death of a man who was her friend and about her own personal struggles with racism.

For a posthumous printing of *I Know Why the Caged Bird*

Sings Oprah Winfrey wrote this, which expresses my understanding of Dr. Angelou: "She understood that sharing her truth connected her to the greater human truths—of longing, abandonment, security, hope, wonder, prejudice, mystery, and, finally, self-discovery: the realization of who you really are and the liberation that love brings."

Not as prominent or honored, but just as valuable a resource are six additional autobiographies published from 1974 to 2002; these trace Dr. Angelou's life until about age 40. (A seventh volume, an "overview," came out in 2013, a year before her death.) All of these volumes are written in a style that came to be called "autobiographical fiction," because of their heavy use of literary devices usually reserved for fiction (including "making things up"). The facts, shaded or not, of her life experiences were fodder for telling stories that engage the imagination. As personal as her words were, they were also universal, because in expressing her experiences, she allowed others to share them.

Autobiographies and memoirs are accounts of a person's life, written in the first person. In that sense, they mean the same thing. Autobiographies, though, generally tell of the complete life, with events in chronological order. Memoirs generally focus more on emotion and interior thoughts. They may be more limited in scope, treating only certain episodes of life and jumping back and forth in time. Angelou's books about herself are a hybrid form that was unique when she started writing them; the form, which includes elements of fiction, has since been adopted by other writers.

She was Marguerite Annie Johnson at birth, April 4, 1928, in St. Louis, Missouri. Her parents were Bailey Johnson, a doorman and Navy dietician, and Vivian Baxter Johnson, a nurse and card dealer. Her brother Bailey was her elder by one year.

The very first words of chapter one of *I Know Why the Caged Bird Sings* tell what happened next to the two little children. Their parents decided to end their rocky marriage, and their father sent them to live with his mother in Arkansas. And so: "When I was three and Bailey four, we had arrived in the musty little town, wearing tags on our wrists which instructed—"To Whom It May Concern"—that we were Marguerite and Bailey Johnson Jr., from Long Beach, California, en route to Stamps, Arkansas, c/o Mrs. Annie Henderson."

Annie Henderson ("Momma" to the children) had run a general store in Stamps ("so prejudiced that a Negro couldn't buy vanilla ice cream") for twenty-five years. The store was central to life in Stamps, and Momma was a community leader. Her original business had been a lunch wagon for workers at the local lumberyard and the cotton gin. Even a single paragraph, this one describing the store, is indicative of Angelou's ability to braid facts, imagination, and metaphor together into indelible images: "Customers could find food staples, a good variety of colored thread, mash for hogs, corn for chickens, coal oil for lamps, light bulbs for the wealthy, shoestrings, hair dressing, balloons, and flower seeds. Anything not visible had only to be ordered. Until we became familiar enough to belong to the Store and it to us, we were locked up in a Fun House of Things where the attendant had gone home for life."

Maya (that's what her brother called her; other people called her Ritie or Margaret or Sister or Mary) and Bailey lived in Stamps for four years. Inexplicably, their father returned and brought them back to St. Louis to live with their mother. There, when Maya was 8 or 9 years old, came the terrible events that, literally, made her mute. When she re-found her voice, nearly half a decade later, it would never be stilled.

Of all the richness that Maya Angelou presents, I want to focus on her *voice*, because it was the foundation of her success. Remember her definition: "Success is loving life and daring to live it."

What follows is the bare outline of what happened to young Maya; the detailed version—which is both lyrical and awful—resides in *I Know Why the Caged Bird Sings.*

Her mother's boyfriend began molesting Maya. The man threatened to kill anyone she told, so she told no one. One day, the man raped her. Maya became so sick and feverish that she was hospitalized; finally, even though she feared the man's threats, she acknowledged to Bailey what had happened. ("He can't kill me. I won't let him," was young Bailey's confident assertion to his sister.) The man was arrested, tried, convicted of rape, and then immediately released. A day later, he was found beaten to death; the assumption was that Maya's uncles had taken revenge. Maya blamed herself for telling both the truth and a lie. The truth was about the rape; the lie was that, when asked at the trial if the man had ever touched her before, she had said no. In her little-girl psyche, speaking was what had caused the man's death. So she stopped speaking. The traumas of the abuse, the rape, and the aftermath silenced her.

"In the first weeks my family accepted my behavior as a post-rape, post-hospital affliction," wrote Angelou. But as soon as she was deemed "healed" (medically, that is), any understanding disappeared: "I was called impudent and my muteness sullenness. For a while I was punished for being so uppity that I wouldn't speak; and then came the thrashings, given by any relative who felt himself offended."

Angelou's exploration of her muteness—from the vantage point of the 40-year-old adult she was when she wrote *I Know Why the Caged Bird Sings*—is heartbreaking: "I had sold myself to the Devil and there would be no escape. They only thing I could do was to stop talking to people, if I talked to anyone else that person might die too."

Soon enough, Maya and Bailey were expelled from St. Louis and on their way back to Stamps: "The barrenness of Stamps was exactly what I wanted. Nothing more could happen. Into this cocoon I crept."

In her time of not speaking, Angelou made an invaluable discovery: "To achieve perfect personal silence all I had to do was to attach myself leechlike to sound.
"I began to listen to everything."

Eventually, time (almost five years), grace, patience, love, and Mrs. Flowers, a teacher and "the lady who threw me my first lifeline," helped bring Maya's voice back. Mrs. Flowers acknowledged Maya's silence and did not shame her for it. Instead, she was gentle with the girl. Most important, Mrs. Flowers presented Maya with a totally new idea: "Language is man's way of communicating with his fellow man and it is language alone which separates him from the lower animals."

Knowing that Maya loved to read, Mrs. Flower noted, "That's good, but not good enough. Words mean more than what is set down on paper. It takes the human voice to infuse them with the shade of deeper meaning."

To demonstrate what it meant "to infuse," Mrs. Flowers took her and Maya's favorite book, *A Tale of Two Cities*, and began to read it aloud. "She opened the first page and I heard poetry for the first time in my life," recounted Maya. It was a new beginning. Thanks to Mrs. Flowers and Maya's discovery of poetry, life could begin again.

Soon after Maya and Bailey graduated from elementary school in 1940, they were back on the road, this time to California, where Vivian was living, first in Los Angeles, later in San

Francisco. By the time Maya graduated from high school, in 1945, she was pregnant from her first consensual sexual encounter, which she initiated. *I Know Why the Caged Bird Sings* ends shortly after her son was born.

The rest of Angelou's progression into adulthood—roughly to the age of 30—can be found in the next three volumes of her autobiography. Those years were a time of building, devoted to supporting her son while at the same time figuring out what her specific strengths were. The remaining volumes take her to age 40, when she initially rebuffs the idea of writing her autobiography—"No, thank you. I am a poet and a playwright." Then rising to the "nearly impossible . . . almost impossible," challenge of writing "autobiography as literature."

In the chapter on Branch Rickey and Jackie Robinson, I talked about Robinson's autobiography, *I Never Had It Made*. Published in 1972, three years after *I Know Why the Caged Bird Sings*, the two books share many themes. Key are the struggles to overcome tragedy and difficulties early in life, to find work, to build relationships, to make one's way in the world. But racism is a primary theme. Robinson expressed his anger about racism, the day-to-day stark reality of it, as did Angelou, who also saw its nuances. On the one hand, when she was 12 years old, Maya was made to feel that "It was awful to be Negro, and to have no control over my life. It was brutal to be young and already trained to sit quietly and listen to charges brought against my color with no chance of defense." On the other hand, this same girl realized, and made it her life's work to fulfill, that "I was a proud member of the wonderful, beautiful Negro race."

Both Jackie Robinson and Maya Angelou received the Presidential Medal of Freedom, the highest civilian award given by the United States. Robinson's recognition came posthumously, in 1984 by Ronald Reagan. Angelou's recognition was in 2010, four years before her death at age 86, by Barack Obama.

★   ★   ★

All the way back in Stamps, Mrs. Flowers had told the young Maya that "you do not love poetry . . . until you speak it." So, it is fitting that, of Dr. Angelou's public appearances, the most well-known may be her recitation of her poem, "On the Pulse of Morning," at President Bill Clinton's first inauguration in 1993. The audio recording of the reading won a Grammy that year for "Best Spoken Word" and helped bring all of her work to broader public attention. One single line in the long poem still calls out to me as Maya Angelou's anthem: "But do not hide your face." She showed us her face, she let us hear her voice.

Maya Angelou was the second poet, and the first woman and first Black poet, to recite at a presidential inauguration ceremony. There have been six such poets to date. JFK started the tradition in 1961 when he invited Robert Frost. Bill Clinton invited Angelou to the 1993 ceremony, Miller Williams to his second, in 1997. For Barack Obama, Elizabeth Alexander read in 2009 and Richard Blanco in 2013. Amanda Gorman was the poet for Joe Biden's inauguration in 2021.

19

AUDREY HEPBURN

(United Kingdom, United States)

I REMEMBER FEELING GENUINE SADNESS, for a woman I didn't know personally, when Audrey Hepburn died on January 20, 1993, at age 63. It wasn't for the superficial reason that she was a very beautiful woman, nor for the more substantial reason that she was a wonderfully talented actress.

No, I felt sorrow because the world had lost a unique humanitarian whose kindness—especially to at-risk, impoverished, and vulnerable children the world over—was profound. And her kindness was concrete; she didn't just feel or wish or think that she should help, she *did* help.

I use the word "lost" to describe the effect on the world when Audrey Hepburn died. Truly, after anyone dies, there is loss. But there is also loss throughout anyone's lived life. In her case, how she endured loss throughout her life gives us insight into how we can respond to loss in ours. (Hint: She kept going.)

Hepburn's oeuvre as an award-winning actress comprised some twenty-six movies and a variety of stage and other performances, including two Broadway plays. Her role as a humanitarian (for which she received the Presidential Medal of Freedom in 1992) was centered on UNICEF, the United Nations Children's Fund, founded in 1946 to help children in the aftermath of World War II. Hepburn, who had donated money to UNICEF and had assisted with projects since her early days of stardom in the 1950s, was appointed an official Goodwill Ambassador in 1988. In the remaining few years of her life, she traveled the world tirelessly for the cause. At the time of her appointment, she said: "I can testify to what UNICEF means to children, because I was among those who received food and medical relief right after World War II."

Her son Sean Ferrer wrote in his 2003 book *Audrey Hepburn, an Elegant Spirit*: "Questions about her youth or her motivations for joining UNICEF would always bring her back to World War II and the hardships she had seen her family and friends live through, the loss of everything we take for granted."

Wrote another biographer: "No other film actress was so revered—inspired and inspiring—both for her on-screen appearances and for her passionate, off-screen crusade."

Indeed, her kindness as an adult was rooted in a singular loss in her childhood and her terrible experiences as an adolescent in WWII, as well as deep personal disappointment in the war's aftermath. Building upon her success as an actress, she made sure those experiences were transformative, for herself and others. How did Hepburn accomplish what she did? In my view, sheer determination; she also shared the same survival instinct as other people in this book.

Born as Audrey ("Adriaantje" to her family) Kathleen Ruston on May 4, 1929, in Brussels, she had a notable international heritage. Her mother, Baroness Ella van Heemstra, was a Dutch noblewoman whose father had served as governor of a Dutch territory abroad; she had been previously married to an oil executive based in the Dutch East Indies. (From her mother's first marriage, Audrey had two half brothers.) Her father, Joseph Ruston, was a British subject who had been born in Austria-Hungary and worked as a trader in the Dutch East Indies; he, too, had been previously married to a Dutch heiress.

Ella and Joseph first lived in the Dutch East Indies, and then returned to Europe. Because of Joseph's work, the family moved among four cities: Brussels and London, as well as The Hague and Arnhem (where Ella's father had served as mayor) in the Netherlands; they finally settled in a suburb of Brussels. As a child, Hepburn spoke Dutch and English at home, and later was fluent in Spanish, French, German, and Italian.

We know her as Audrey *Hepburn* because, after her birth, her father modified his name to Hepburn-Ruston, to reflect a possible historic ancestor; she later dropped the "Ruston." And speaking of names, if you're wondering if she and another famous actress, Katharine Hepburn, were related, the answer is no.

Audrey's life—sheltered and privileged—was jolted when she was 6 years old. Her father, who had become a Fascist activist, abruptly left the family, moved to London, and never returned. Other children have had this loss, but even if it is common, we cannot discount its impact.

Her mother sent Audrey's half brothers to live with relatives in The Hague and took Audrey with her to the van Heemstra estate in Arnhem. At age 8, because of Joseph's insistence that Audrey be educated in England, she was sent to a boarding school in Kent. When Britain declared war on Germany in 1939, Ella brought Audrey back to the ancestral home in Arnhem, assuming that the Netherlands, historically a neutral country, would be a safe haven. As we all know, it was not to be.

Ten-year-old Audrey, who had begun studying ballet at her boarding school, was enrolled at the Arnhem Conservatory, where she continued her dance training as a "star pupil." There was a semblance of normalcy, but short-lived, as the Germans invaded the Netherlands in 1940. Life under the five-year occupation began for 11-year-old Audrey, her mother, her teen-age half brothers, and her extended Dutch family. Thus com-menced her version of World War II loss: again, not the same as others' greater losses, but shared losses just the same.

Let's fast-forward some fifty years in the future to 1990, to a UNICEF benefit program in Chicago when Hepburn narrated *From the Diary of Anne Frank*, a work composed and conducted by Michael Tilson Thomas and performed by his New World Symphony. Here is part of what Hepburn said: "Anne Frank and I were born in the same year, lived in the same country, experienced the same war, except that she was locked up and I was on the outside . . . All the events I experienced were so in-credibly accurately described by her—not just what was going on, on the outside, but what was going on inside of a young girl starting to become a woman . . . all in a cage."

Anne Frank did not survive the war, as we know; she died in February or March 1945 in the Bergen-Belsen concentration camp. Audrey did survive, yet the extreme privations she and her family had experienced during the occupation affected her for the rest of her life. Chief among the hardships was the scarcity of food. Her son Sean Ferrer wrote, "She told us about how her brothers ate dog biscuits when there was nothing else to eat, how others ate tulip bulbs, and how bread was green be-cause the only flour available was made from peas."

Because of the dire shortage of food and because they thought it would be safer outside the city when heavy bombing started, the family moved to her grandfather's home in the sub-urbs. The family also thought that food would be easier to ob-tain once they were closer to farmlands. But the farmers in the region were just scraping by themselves because they were shar-ing what little they had with people in the city.

There were also the sights the young Audrey could never un-see. Sean Ferrer cited just two: "Families of Jews being loaded onto trains, and how she could never forget the vision of one little girl wearing a red coat disappearing into the gaping doors of a cattle car." An uncle and a cousin were executed by the Nazis; one of her brothers was sent to a labor camp and the other went into hiding.

Audrey's family was among those who lost everything (in material terms, not their spirits) in the war. The ancestral van Heemstra properties were confiscated or destroyed, and in 1945 Ella began working as a domestic for a wealthy family in Amsterdam. Even so, she was able to keep up Audrey's dance education, because to be a prima ballerina was the girl's dream.

In 1948, Audrey won a scholarship to the Ballet Rambert, a leading British company run by a protégé of the great Nijinsky, but it was soon evident that "the war had stolen her dream." Too many of the years that are crucial in a young dancer's development had gone by when she was unable to train, and the privations of the war had impaired the growth of her muscles. Furthermore, she was competing in Britain against other young dancers who had been able to carry on their training during the war. It was little consolation to Audrey that she was told that although being "first ballerina" was out of her reach, she could have a good career as a "second ballerina" and as a teacher.

Thwarted in her dream but very realistic and goal-oriented, at age 19 "she had to go on and make a living," wrote her son. (Remember that her mother, the baroness who believed in her, was working as a domestic.) "If it wasn't going to be ballet, if she couldn't be the best dancer, she would be the best at something else." Hepburn thus turned her attention and her ambition away from her loss. She looked to the profession of acting—and became "the best."

Think about a dream you have had and lost, perhaps one that someone else dashed. Did you accept their judgment? Maybe they knew more than you did about what it would take for fulfillment. Maybe they didn't. How did you move on? Did you set a new goal? Have you ever had to counsel someone to follow plan B instead of plan A?

Audrey Hepburn made it look almost effortless, her path to accomplishment. But she was determined; she *worked* at her new craft. As she did, role after supporting role—some of them quite minor, to be sure—came her way as British and French casting directors took notice of her unaffected appeal. In 1951, when she was just 22 and filming a small role in Monte Carlo, she was spotted by the novelist Colette, who cast her as the star of *Gigi*, a play being developed for Broadway by Anita Loos based on Collette's 1944 novel of the same name.

Now Hepburn was on her way to fame in the United States and beyond. *Gigi* ran for 219 performances in New York—garnering Hepburn a Theatre World Award for her work and a favorable *New York Times* notice: "Her quality is so winning and so right that she is the success of the evening." *Gigi* toured for seven months through Pittsburgh, Cleveland, Chicago, Detroit, Washington, and Los Angeles. By the time the play closed in May 1953, Audrey Hepburn had caught the eye of Hollywood. That same year, she starred with Gregory Peck in *Roman Holiday*, winning, for her work, Oscar and Golden Globe awards for best actress, and the BAFTA award for best British actress. There was no doubt of the direction of her career. At age 24, she was securely on her way to being "the best."

In 1952, Hepburn had a supporting role as a ballerina in *The Secret People*, in which she performed three dancing sequences. Though the film received decidedly mixed reviews, it led, along with *Gigi*, to her breakthrough role in *Roman Holiday*.

Hepburn worked prodigiously, but very naturally and gracefully in all her film roles, throughout the 1950s and 1960s. She "slowed down" in the 1970s to spend more time on her private life—which included the losses of miscarriages and failed marriages—but her work as a performer continued well into the 1980s.

By the time she shifted her attention—and her energy—to

UNICEF, she had attained the professional goal she had set for herself when she was 19. She was beloved by the public. There was no professional award—Oscar, Tony, Emmy, and Grammy among them—she did not win, sometimes multiple times. She even received two awards for work that debuted posthumously.

Hepburn was married twice, to the actor Mel Ferrer and the psychiatrist Andrea Dotti, and had two sons. In the last dozen years of her life, her companion was the actor Robert Wolders, whose encouragement was instrumental in her becoming a UNICEF Special Ambassador. In a "you can't make this up" scenario, he had been a child in a different suburb of Arnhem during the war and his experiences of survival were very similar to Hepburn's.

And now to what I think is the key to appreciating Audrey Hepburn—her kindness as expressed through UNICEF. She could have been satisfied by what she had already accomplished: She was "the best," as she had urged herself to be when she was a disappointed teenager whose dream had been stripped away. But as befits an actress, the curtain soon rose on her final act.

UNICEF had helped save Audrey Hepburn in the aftermath of Holland's crippling five-year occupation. The war might have been over, but the suffering of the people continued. Sean Ferrer quoted his mother as reminiscing: "Food dwindled . . . whatever there was went to the troops. There's a big difference between dying of starvation and malnutrition, of course, but I was very, very undernourished."

After the war, the forerunner of UNICEF in cooperation with the Red Cross brought in food, medicines, and clothes for the desperate, starving Dutch. One of the beneficiaries was Audrey Hepburn, and she never forgot it. "I've known about UNICEF all my life," she said.

In 1988, Hepburn was installed as a "Goodwill Ambassador" as part of a program (still ongoing to this day) to harness celebrities to draw attention to UNICEF's international work among at-risk children.

American readers of a certain age will remember the little orange box, like a miniature milk carton, that we would carry around with us on Halloween. In addition to begging for candy, we would collect pennies, nickels, and dimes—sometimes even a quarter—as we went from house to house in the neighborhood, showing off our costumes. "Trick or Treat for UNICEF," which began as a homespun effort in Philadelphia in 1950, continues even today—virtually, of course, as in-person Halloweens have fallen away for many reasons. It was cited by the Nobel committee as one of the reasons that UNICEF received the Peace Prize in 1965.

In her very first year as an ambassador, Hepburn accompanied UNICEF teams and government officials to Ethiopia, Turkey, Venezuela, Ecuador, Guatemala, Mexico, Honduras, El Salvador, and Sudan. Her international travels continued at that same brisk pace, even through the last year of her life, when she was ill with her fatal cancer.

This description from UNICEF gives a snapshot of how she handled the job: "Soon after becoming a UNICEF ambassador, Hepburn went on a mission to Ethiopia, where years of drought and civil strife had caused terrible famine . . . She talked about the projects to the media in the United States, Canada, and Europe over several weeks, giving as many as 15 interviews a day. It set a precedent for her commitment to the organization."

In the years that followed, Hepburn made many more field trips, including to a polio vaccine project in Turkey, training programs for women in Venezuela, projects for children living on the streets in Ecuador, and drinking water programs in Guatemala and Honduras. She visited schools in Bangladesh, nutrition projects in Vietnam, and camps for displaced children in Sudan.

Because of her star power, Hepburn was also a tireless and highly effective advocate for UNICEF. She testified before Congress, took part in the World Summit for Children, launched UNICEF's "State of the World's Children" reports, hosted the Danny Kaye International Children's Award ceremonies, took part in benefit concerts, gave speeches, and conducted countless interviews. And if that wasn't enough, she also designed UNICEF's fundraising cards.

I began this chapter thinking about the death—the loss—of a very determined woman, Audrey Hepburn. None of us are immortal, of course, but there are ways that we live on; through our families and friends, for example. And a woman such as Hepburn inspires us to think about how we respond to loss in our own lives.

An actress such as Hepburn is in a unique position to live on because we can summon up her films at any time on the "devices" that connect us to the internet, where nothing seems to die. We can remind ourselves of her beauty, her talent, her freshness, her appeal, the complexity that existed in a deceptively simple package. A humanitarian such as Hepburn also lives on—in her case because others continue her work through their own philanthropy for UNICEF and other causes.

20

RUDOLF NUREYEV
(Russia)

Few of us have provoked an international crisis at age 23. Few of us would go that far in an effort to attain artistic and personal freedom. Rudolf Nureyev did so, on May 19, 1961, when he defected from the Soviet Union. Rejecting Communism, he lived to tell the tale, and then some.

The first Soviet artist to defect to the West during the Cold War, Nureyev attained the height of fame, accomplishment, and sensation as one of the two or three greatest male dancers of the twentieth century. Acclaim also surrounded him as a director, teacher, and choreographer—and popular icon.

The pleasure and privilege of seeing Nureyev perform was unforgettable. I recall being mesmerized by his astonishing leaps and flights and spins across New York's Lincoln Center stage when I first saw him dance in the 1970s. How could a person move that way? With beautiful athleticism, he challenged the laws of gravity and physics. His balletic gifts were sublime.

Why does Rudolf Nureyev command our attention now, more than sixty years after his historic defection and three decades after his death? I'll turn to Clive Barnes, the British theater/dance critic, who followed Nureyev's entire career and was one of his biographers. He said simply, "Nureyev changed the face of ballet."

Many questions surround the dancer's defection and remain valid today. Chief among them: Was his action political or personal? Was he truly rebelling against Communism, against all authoritarianism? Or was he merely tired of strictures that kept him from pursuing his own selfish pleasures? Was his defection a one-off, or did he inspire others to do the same?

These questions and any possible answers are eclipsed by the brilliance of his talent, which may well have been lost to the world had he remained in the Soviet system.

There are two additional questions that I wish I could pose to Nureyev directly and hear his own answers in his own voice. Think about them as you read what follows:

- Were you running toward something, or running away?
- Were you dancing someone else's composition, or choreographing your own?

I decided to include Nureyev in this book because he was a brave man. As much as he chafed under Communism, it was all he knew. At age 23, he took a definitive risk to move from that life—characterized by control and conformity—toward an unknown life that he hoped would offer the freedom he craved.

Nureyev knowingly made a political statement by rejecting his country and its system. But politics was not his impetus. As he himself wrote: "I see nothing political in the necessity for a young artist to see the world: to compare, assimilate, to enrich his art with new experiences."

The facts of Nureyev's biography and his contributions to the world of dance are objective and easily researched. Yes, he was great. What is more interesting, to me and I hope to you, is to imagine the motivations and emotions that surrounded his defection. What led the young Soviet man to commit to that irreversible decision; what did it feel like to carry it out?

I have been helped in that quest by reading his autobiography, written in 1962, just a year after his "leap" to freedom.

The contemporaneous account of what happened is very compelling, very subjective, and undoubtedly propagandistic— Nureyev knew how to play that game. Reading the book deepened my view of Nureyev. No longer a mere fan, I now have a fuller appreciation of his human complexity.

Does Nureyev's defection still matter? Yes, I believe it does. It was a deeply individual act with universal meaning.

On an individual level, it showed how the young Nureyev would go on to live his life always seeking freedom. The last two sentences of his autobiography, written a year into his post-defection life, tell us: "I don't want to be told where my proper future lies, what is the 'right' way to develop. I shall try to find this out for myself. That is what I mean by freedom."

On a universal human level, his craving strikes a chord with all of us, at any age. Freedom is a deep-seated human need. Those who stifle it in others do them a grave wrong. Those who stifle it in themselves do not live full lives. For something so lofty and beautiful, though, freedom has feet of clay. Pursuing it can hurt us and those we love. It is delicate, like a scalpel; it is powerful, like a bludgeon. I think Nureyev knew all this.

Freedom was specifically necessary for Nureyev in 1961 because without it, his dancing career would have ceased to exist. As we will see, at the time of his defection the authorities were preparing to force an end to his young career.

But dancing was more than livelihood for him. Its movements formed the core of his identity. Dancing became his passion, his reason for living, when he was 7 years old, when "the time was drawing near for my real, unique passion to invade my heart, my body and my whole life." His obituary in *The New York Times* said, "Life and dance were one" for him. Without freedom, life and dance could not exist for Nureyev.

We've examined other luminaries in this book who lived with passion. Most were able to do so safely, without impediment. Nureyev's story beckoned to me, for this book, because it was surrounded by danger. It also beckoned because—again, like some other people in this book—he had no idea that he was nearly halfway through his life when he made history. He died in 1993 at age 54. Even so, he outlived the Soviet Union, which dissolved in 1991.

At the time of his defection in 1961, Nureyev was in Paris on tour with the famed Kirov Ballet of Leningrad, whose school he had entered at age 17 after he emerged from the distant provinces of the USSR with only rudimentary dance experience. Amazingly, he was already a soloist. The tour was the third time the Soviet authorities had permitted him to leave the country; the previous year had seen brief trips with the Kirov to Vienna and Berlin.

Six years into his meteoric ballet career, his talent blossoming, Nureyev was notorious on- and off-stage—always the center of attention, independent, defiant of all authority. His autobiography details many instances of his "rebellion" and "insolence," along with an overwhelming sense of being oppressed. Accounts by others say the same thing. Instances of official retaliation against the young dancer—because of his behavior and sometimes for no reason at all—were common. His personality would not change, ever. Unruly was a descriptor that turned up in media profiles over the years, along with charismatic, temperamental, unpredictable, passionate, arrogant, and narcissistic. His complex personality was founded on contradictions. He could be charming and be rude, good-humored and sullen, innocent and crafty.

Time in Vienna and Berlin, though quite limited, had given him hints of what life could be like . . . elsewhere. The cities had introduced him to a world beyond the constraints of life in a Communist country. Now, in Paris, the world was being introduced to a young man who would go on to dance like no one since the legendary Nijinsky earlier in the century.

To say that twenty-something Nureyev made the authorities nervous would be an understatement. On the one hand, he was a rising star in the Communist solar system, beginning to light up the world. He had burst on the scene in the early years of space exploration, and the press turned to that for metaphors. One French paper exulted, "The Kirov has found its cosmonaut: Rudolf Nureyev!" Other French critics called him "a Sputnik" after the first Russian satellite.

On the other hand, he was breaking away from the *kollectiv* on his way to becoming his own universe. Already showing greatness, he was on the way to even more greatness. He was too individual. He needed to be contained.

The Cold War began immediately after World War II, rooted in the "mutually assured destruction" approach taken by Eastern and Western bloc countries. It featured, among many other restrictions, prohibitions of people's ability to travel freely across borders. The 1991 dissolution of the Soviet Union marked its end. In place of military aggression, "softer" competition in sports, science, and the arts became the hallmark of relations between the United States and the USSR. Any defection to the West was seen as a rejection of the Soviet system that depended on control of the people and obedience to the state. Defections of athletes, scientists, and artists were seen as especially dangerous.

At Le Bourget (then the international airport near Paris) that day in May 1961, the dance troupe was ready to board the airplane that would take them on to London, the next stop on their tour. Nureyev, however, was separated from his colleagues by KGB agents and ordered to wait for another plane— the one back to Moscow. The ruse was that he was needed to dance at a special gala for Premier Nikita Khrushchev, but Nureyev knew better.

The time had come for Nureyev to face the inevitable. It was utterly predictable that he would be pulled back, like a recalcitrant dog on a leash. Was his action in response also inevitable? I believe the answer is "Yes." Defection was not an impetuous act, rooted in youth and immaturity. But even if it happened "in the moment," it was a rational, natural outgrowth of his life's experiences.

Nureyev himself had long harbored dreams of what "freedom" would really mean. He had spoken about the concept of defection to his friends and associates in terms both open and veiled. Was he ready to take such a dangerous step? If he succeeded, where would he go; what would happen to his mother and father and sisters? Trying to defect, and failing, would be close to fatal—if not for his life, certainly for his art; again, his family would be made to suffer. Yet he also had a very clear idea what the repercussions might be if he surrendered his will to the authorities and returned to his country. He would not be rewarded for being a "good" Communist, a good Soviet. Banishment back to the provinces, retaliation against his family, even imprisonment—all were possible.

Though our circumstances might not have been so dire, we all have faced moments such as this. Or we will. When the status quo cannot be maintained and any possible action seems, well, impossible. When the solution seems more perilous than the problem.

"The possibility continued to preoccupy him—it was just courage to carry it out that he lacked," observed his biographer Julie Kavanagh in her monumental work *Nureyev*. A dancer who certainly knew how to take a step, whose leaps and flights across the ballet stage were extraordinary—Nureyev was paralyzed. It wasn't just an absence of courage. He also lacked an actual plan, unlike fellow Russian dancer Mikhail Baryshnikov, who would defect in 1974 after four years of meticulous plotting.

At the crowded, chaotic airport that day—full of travelers, onlookers, friends, enemies, agents, police, suspicion, fear—"I was like a bird inside a net being drawn tighter and tighter," wrote Nureyev. "I felt I would rather kill myself . . . I thought to myself: This is the end."

Nureyev, plan-less and in an act of sheer courage, refused to comply with the KGB agents and made himself known to two French policemen. Julie Kavanagh wrote drily of the moment: "Then Rudolf walked slowly—'six steps exactly'—directly up to the two French commissars . . . [and said] 'I would like to stay in your country.'"

Nureyev's autobiographical account is rather more dramatic. He called it "the longest, most breath-taking leap of my whole career," adding, "I landed squarely in the arms of the two inspectors. 'I want to stay,' I gasped. 'I want to stay.'"

Rudolf Nureyev was the first dancer to defect during the Cold War, but he was not the only one. Most visible were Mikhail Baryshnikov in 1974 and Alexander Godunov in 1979. The pre-eminent choreographer and New York City Ballet founder George Balanchine, with whom both Nureyev and Baryshnikov worked, was also a defector—in 1924, at age 20. All said the same—art and freedom drove them, not politics.

In his adolescence, he was dubbed "the white crow" because of his singularity. Rudolf Khametovich Nureyev certainly had an unusual start. He was born on March 17, 1938, in Irkutsk, Siberia, in the USSR—on a crowded military transport train as it circled Lake Baikal. Many years ago, I visited Irkutsk; when talking with people in restaurants and other public places, I heard the name Nureyev repeated time after time.

His nearly full-term pregnant mother Farida had been ordered to travel with her three young daughters to join her husband Hamet, serving yet another new assignment with the Red Army's Far Eastern Division in Vladivostok. The weeks-long trip across the vast Siberian countryside was risky but, in a way, enjoyable. The family was nestled among other military dependents, the children sleeping in bunks in the passenger cars as if in summer camp. Farida was getting good medical attention. Her new baby was greeted with joy and amazement by his fellow travelers.

Then and there, the Nureyev mystique was also born. Julie Kavanagh related, "Word of the event spread quickly, and for the rest of the day people crowded into the carriage to see the new arrival: Rudolf Nureyev's first audience."

Nureyev, in his autobiography, told the story as well. Not that he *remembered* his birth—that would really have made him a "white crow!"—but he embraced its symbolic circumstances: "I always think of my birth as the most romantic event of my life."

I want to pause here to honor Nureyev's attraction to trains, which he linked to his lifelong pursuit of freedom, dance, and movement. Not the toy trains that so many children play with and eventually outgrow, nor the adult hobby involving elaborate scaled models and layouts—real trains. I think this trait is important to understanding Nureyev at the time of his defection.

Nicknamed *malchik kotoriy rodilsay v poesde* ("the boy who was born on a train"), the infant Rudik "would be lulled to sleep by the sound of trains rattling along the track beyond the back fence," wrote Kavanagh.

Nureyev wrote that when he was a little older, he liked to sit "motionless" on a hill above railroad tracks near his home in Ufa "simply watching the trains slowly starting and getting up speed. I loved the sensation of being driven somewhere else by those wheels." It is easy to see how such sounds and sensations would become embodied in the boy and foster a love of movement, as both a dancer and a "vagabond soul."

When he was in Leningrad with the Kirov, "before creating

a role in a new ballet I would often go to the station and just look, until I could feel the movement become part of me, and I part of the train. That helped me somehow in my dancing though I can't say exactly how." And later, at Le Bourget, when his luggage and all its contents would be lost in the fog of defection—"most of all I regretted [losing] my very first purchase in Paris—a beautiful electric train."

The romanticism of his birth aside, the boy's early life—actually, most of his young life—was not easy. Few people's lives were easy in that time and place, and children were not exempt.

Rudik came from a family of peasants—ethnically, they were Tatar Muslims hailing from Bashkir, in the Ural Mountains where Eastern Europe meets North Asia—who were also proud Communists. His father Hamed joined the Red Army as an instructor who was often abruptly transferred from one posting to another. The parents' marriage was not smooth due to Hamed's domineering nature and the pressures of military life.

A toddler when war came in June 1941, Rudik essentially had no father in his life for the next five years. He was almost 8 when Hamed, having accepted a yearlong transfer to Germany after the war ended in 1945 rather than return home, finally reappeared. Hamed had been summarily demoted and then discharged from the army, in spite of having won several medals and citations for meritorious service. During Hamed's long absence, poverty and the dangers of war had marked the life of Farida and her children. *Bomsch* ("beggar") was a slur frequently hurled at them. Potatoes were their subsistence, and Rudik would often faint from hunger. After their house was bombed, the family fled back to Bashkir, to its capital city of Ufa.

"It was a disillusioned and bitter man who returned . . . to a family to whom he was virtually a stranger," said Kavanagh. Nureyev remembered him as "an unknown force that rarely smiled, rarely spoke and who scared me. Even in my teens I still felt afraid to look at him directly."

War-related absences and returns were not an unusual experience for any family at that time. Add in poverty and difficult personalities and disillusions. We absorb experiences in our own unique ways, and these experiences accumulate with others that may or may not be remarkable but that form our character. Unhappily back home with his family after the humiliating end of his army career, Hamed brought his authoritarian nature, honed by commanding and being commanded in the army, to bear on his son. It's easy to see where the roots of Rudik's lifelong rebellion might lie.

And it's easy to see—aside from trains—where his passion for dance might have come from. Movement ran in his blood because of the Russian heritage of folk dance, whose steps, rhythms, and music Rudik began learning at a very young age. And there was, as is so often the case, the influence of his mother. One formative experience involved the single ticket that Farida had been given to a special New Year's Eve ballet performance at the Ufa Opera House—she smuggled all four children in with her. Nureyev never forgot the "sorcery" of that night: "There was simply from this quite early age the awareness that the only thing I wanted was to dance."

He may have wanted to dance, but the circumstances of his life—poverty, limited opportunity in general, lingering privations from the war, his father's opposition, few teachers, his provincial existence far from the metropolitan centers of his country where he could really learn—were daunting. But they did not crush Nureyev's spirit or talent or extinguish his passion. He was finally able, at age 17, to make his way alone to Leningrad and to an academy affiliated with the Kirov Ballet, where his peers were students who had been studying ballet seriously for eight or nine years already. By age 20, he was a soloist at the Kirov Ballet itself and three years after that, he made history at Le Bourget.

Did Russians invent ballet? No and yes. The dance form dates to early in the Renaissance, originating in Italy as a theatrical art aligned with opera and court dance; it spread to France and thence throughout Europe. (The French word "ballet," which we use in English as well, comes from *ballare*—"to dance"—in Italian.) In the 1700s, Peter the Great brought ballet to Russia as part of his effort to Westernize Russia, and the classic "Russian style" came to dominate the art. Up until the early 1800s, men were the leading ballet dancers, but then the role of the ballerina became more important. One of Nureyev's many innovations was to reclaim the preeminent role of the male dancer—at least in the work he could control through his own choreography. For example, his interpretation of *Swan Lake* non-traditionally emphasized the role of Prince Siegfried over that of the Odette/Odile ballerina.

In his autobiography, Nureyev tells this story: Just before he was to take the stage in his first post-defection performance, messages were delivered to him from his mother and his father. In a telegram, his mother begged him to come home. In a letter, his father told him there was "no excuse" for what he had done to "betray his fatherland." There was also a letter from his mentor that "was shattering." Nureyev knew that the timing of these messages was not accidental but was designed by the Soviets to derail him. He knew that his parents, if not his mentor, were being used as propaganda tools. He wrote: "Someone in authority had understood very well that the only weapon that could wound me and make me come back was the thought of my parents' anxiety. Their anguish affected me deeply."

Yet not enough to deflect him from his path, his life, his passion. He danced that night, and ever after. In the *Los Angeles Times*, he was quoted thusly: "I love my mother, I sometimes talk to her on the telephone. But the old life means very little to me and I push all such thoughts away. I have never regretted that I chose to leave Russia."

He only ever returned to the USSR on a forty-eight-hour visa in 1987 to see his mother near the end of her life.

Earlier, I said that exercising one's freedom can hurt others. One of the many complications of Nureyev's defection was that it hurt, permanently, those he left behind in the USSR. One of his sisters, for example, eventually suffered a mental breakdown thought to be connected to his action. This is a lesson to all of us as we contemplate the moves we will take in our lives. "No man is an island"—John Donne's words have myriad implications.

In spite of his bravado, at a time of great peril after his defection, Nureyev had become a man without a country. But because he was so prominent, everyone knew what had happened. His friends, supporters, fans were legion. Essentially, he was protected. And he continued his career almost without missing a beat.

Nureyev never permanently aligned with any of the more than sixteen ballet companies he danced with. He preferred always to be a guest dancer/choreographer/artistic director/conductor, roaming the world as he did so. Nor did he align with any one country until he became a citizen of Austria in 1982. ("To me, a country is just a place to dance in," he once said, though he traveled under protective papers of transit from Monaco for some years.) Austria's capital had been the first stop of his very first international tour from the USSR in 1960. "Both as an artist and as a person, I like Vienna and the Viennese," he told the media when his citizenship was announced. "I am grateful to a country which historically has a great tradition in welcoming and integrating foreigners." And he may have been a nomad, but he was never homeless, with numerous residences all over the world.

As if his secure place in the pantheon of great classical dancers onstage was not enough, Nureyev also became a cultural darling off-stage. He went nowhere without an entourage. His hair styles, fashion choices, and other affectations were scrutinized and then emulated. He appeared in films and toured with a Broadway musical revival. Ed Sullivan, a "star-maker" who often had professional dance companies appear on his eponymous TV show, showcased Nureyev and Dame Margot Fonteyn. He was photographed by Richard Avedon. He was a muse for the painter Jamie Wyeth. And no one who saw it can forget *The Muppet Show* episode when he performed opposite Miss Piggy in "Swine Lake."

Everyone deserves privacy, and I am not going to draw back the curtain on Nureyev's sexuality. As he was quoted, without elaboration, "Of course I have a personal life." He lived . . . flamboyantly. His homosexuality was an open secret at a time when such an identity was still held as a secret; he may have been bisexual. He had several scandalous liaisons with women early on, and his personal/professional relationship with the great ballerina Dame Margot Fonteyn was inscrutable, though he admitted, "We danced with one body, one soul. She is all I have, only her." In his adulthood, he had long personal partnerships with Erik Bruhn and Robert Tracy, both prominent dancers.

Obituaries written at the time of Nureyev's death cite "a cardiac complication, following a grievous illness" as cause of his death January 6, 1993, though it was obvious to all that complications from AIDS were the reality. Nureyev was long thought to have had AIDS, but he never openly acknowledged his condition. Progressively weaker and more emaciated, so sick, he still danced on, living the life he chose. It was fitting that he was last seen in public—very briefly, for he was so frail—being honored at a gala. Over the years, Nureyev had been quoted as saying: "The main thing is dancing, and before it withers from my body, I will keep dancing until the last moment, the last drop. You live as long as you dance."

As with so many prominent people, it's useful to turn to published obituaries for succinct summations of lives and accomplishments—and foibles:

- *Washington Post:* "Nureyev was a magnetic performer who was credited with redefining the role of the male dancer . . . the embodiment of the true romantic, rootless and alone, willing to place art above all."
- *New York Times:* "He immediately became one of ballet's chief popularizers through his contemporary approach to the 19th century classics. His personal obsession with dance was well known, inspiring him to master a bewildering variety of styles and to embark on never-ending tours."
- *Los Angeles Times:* "He possessed an uncanny memory, which enabled him to dance a role after seeing it once, an ability that simplified his appearance with so many different ballet companies."
- *Los Angeles Times* obituary also quoted music and dance critic Martin Bernheimer: "At his lofty best, he was a serious, probing artist. At his willful worst, he could be infuriatingly narcissistic. Even at his worst, however, he all but dared the viewer not to watch him and, by inference, not to love him."

At the beginning of this chapter, I posed a number of questions about Nureyev's defection and opined about the meaning of freedom and passion in his life. Remember the questions I wished I could pose directly to him? Well, now I will restate them a bit and ask you to think about them in the context of your own life, decisions, passions—as I have for myself many times:

- Were you/are you running toward something, or running away?
- Were you/are you living a life that someone else designed for you, or making your own?

21

SALLY RIDE AND CHRISTA MCAULIFFE

(United States)

TWO YOUNG WOMEN SOUGHT TO MAKE HISTORY for the most positive of reasons. One lived doing so. One died.

They each claimed a "first" in the annals of space travel, in the ongoing exploration of the universe beyond the limits of the earth's atmosphere. Astronaut Sally Ride was the first American woman to fly into space. Teacher Christa McAuliffe was the first "ordinary citizen" to fly into space.

Though their time at NASA overlapped only briefly, they are forever bound together in our imaginations, along with the space shuttle *Challenger*, the vessel on which they traveled, on separate missions.

Sally Ride went into space twice during her nine-year NASA career: in 1983 (when she was 32 years old and happened to be NASA's youngest astronaut, another first) and 1984. For each voyage, she was a crew member on the *Challenger*. As 1986 began, she was training for her third mission, scheduled to take place after *Challenger*'s then-current mission, Christa McAuliffe's mission. One of the goals of NASA's shuttle program was to emulate the near-continuous use of commercial aircraft, which fly, arrive, are serviced, and fly again.

Another one of NASA's goals was, frankly, good public relations. The agency wanted to increase excitement about, and support for, space flight and the science behind it. Opening up possibilities to a broader audience was a key strategy. That's why Christa McAuliffe, a teacher and a civilian, was on the *Challenger* that day that we all remember, January 28, 1986. All seven crew aboard were killed when the shuttle launched, soared into the sky, and exploded after a seventy-three-second flight. McAuliffe was 38 years old.

The shuttle program was immediately suspended, resuming after two years. Dr. Ride was chosen to serve on the board that investigated the *Challenger* disaster. (Almost twenty years later, when the shuttle *Columbia* disintegrated upon re-entry into earth's atmosphere, again killing an entire crew of seven, she was part of that investigation as well.)

Sally Ride the scientist. Christa McAuliffe the teacher. Both these two young thirty-something women had prepared themselves well for their careers—neither of which was to include traveling to what used to be called, quaintly, "outer space." What brought them to NASA and to the "firsts" that were turning points in their lives?

> I can find no evidence that Sally and Christa ever met, even though their time at NASA overlapped. If they did not know each other, though, they must have known of each other. If they ever talked, do you think they focused on the identity of being "first," which is often more important to onlookers than to the people involved, or to the joy they found in space exploration. Or other, more mundane topics?

Sally Ride was 26 years old in 1977, about to receive her PhD in astrophysics from Stanford University; only her thesis remained to be written. With three other degrees from Stanford (BA in English with a concentration in Shakespeare, BS in physics, MS in physics), she clearly was oriented toward a life in academia. Soon she would be applying for teaching positions.

One morning, drinking coffee and getting ready for the day, she read an article in the daily student newspaper with the headline "NASA to Recruit Women"—and not just women for any old NASA job, but for the first time as pilots and mission specialists—as *astronauts*. And it was not just women who were being newly recruited, there was a focus on minorities as well. And on *scientists*. The NASA era of astronauts being exclusively White-men-with-military-flying-experience was ending.

Ride decided—almost instantaneously—to apply. As Lynn Sherr, journalist and friend, subsequently reported: " 'I just had this Wow! feeling,' Sally later said. 'I read through the list of requirements for mission specialist and said to myself, I could do that.' "

Dr. Ride would be part of the new NASA era. Out of eight thousand applicants, she was one of thirty-five people to be chosen for the first new class, which included six White women, three Black men, and one Asian-American man. In early 1978, she entered NASA training as a mission specialist. (Sadly, one sister-member of her class of astronauts, Dr. Judith Resnik, was a crewmate on the *Challenger* with Christa McAuliffe.)

The "space race" was one of the defining elements of the post-WWII Cold War between the United States and the Soviet Union. With the successful launch of the (unmanned) satellite *Sputnik 1* in 1957, the Soviets were ahead in the race, and it was imperative that the United States not only catch up but exceed. Citizens were nervous about Soviets "flying around up there." National security was at stake. What's called the "Pearl Harbor effect" came urgently into play, with new funding, new agencies, new coordination among existing agencies, new R&D efforts.

Early in 1958 the United States launched its first satellite, the *Explorer*, and, later in the year, the NASA organization was formalized. Its official goal was "to provide for research into the problems of flight within and outside Earth's atmosphere, and for other purposes." "Other purposes" indeed; defense of the country was never far from anyone's mind.

Within three years, the space race was neck and neck. The Soviets sent the first man into space in April 1961, the Americans in May 1961. The missions met their objectives; cosmonaut Yuri Gagarin and astronaut Alan Shepard returned safely to Earth.

In July 1970, the space race ended when American astronaut Neil Armstrong became the first person to step onto the moon; in July 1975, joint American–Soviet/Russian space missions commenced and continue to this day. (The Cold War officially ended in 1991 when the Soviet Union was dissolved.)

American-manned space travel was centered around the Mercury program (1961–63), Project Gemini (1965–66), and Project Apollo (1968–72), augmented by unmanned satellite exploration. Each successive program built on the previous one in all ways, but a characteristic of each spacecraft was that it was single use, burning up (with the obvious exception of the astronaut's "pod") in Earth's atmosphere as it returned from space. And each astronaut—a man with military experience—reflected NASA's role in American national security apparatus.

The goal of diversifying the NASA astronaut cadre had been bandied about since the early 1960s, but it was impetus from President Nixon in 1972 that had formalized the effort. Post-*Apollo*, the next generation of spacecraft was emerging. The new Space Transport System—a "shuttle fleet for low Earth orbit"—would be made up of reusable vessels capable of frequent and long-lasting flights, whose crews did lots of experiments.

After testing using the vessel *Enterprise* in 1977, the Space Transport System flew 135 missions over its thirty-year duration. Five vessels comprised the active fleet: *Columbia* (launched in 1981 and lost in 2003), *Challenger* (launched in 1983 and lost in 1986), *Discovery* (launched in 1984), *Atlantis* (launched in 1985), and *Endeavor* (launched in 1992). The last mission was in July 2011.

By its very nature, the STS would offer more "jobs" on its frequent shuttle missions, more complex jobs, and thus more opportunities for pilots, specialists, and technicians of all kinds. The time was more than ripe for changes of all sorts. In 1976, the new diversification program was announced. Sally Ride found out about it the next year, pretty much accidentally as no advisor had steered her toward it.

When she was in her mid-twenties, in the mid-1970s, Christa McAuliffe seemed on track, leading the life she had planned for: to be a wife, to be a teacher, to be a mother.

She had graduated college in 1970 with a major in history and had moved from her hometown of Framingham, Massachusetts, to the Washington, D.C., area with her husband Steven (high school sweetheart!), who had entered Georgetown University Law School. She was teaching high-school-level history and civics, waitressing part-time, and studying for an MA in teaching administration. By the end of the decade, Christa and Steven would have two children and would return to New England, settling in Concord, New Hampshire. Along with her husband, then an assistant attorney general in state government, she was a full-fledged participant in the challenging world of combining career and family.

Importantly for her pioneering future role as a "teacher in space," McAuliffe was an adventurous teacher. Sure, she followed established social studies curricula, but she also brought "nontraditional" visitors into the classroom, almost as guest teachers. She often took her students out of the classroom on field trips and designed a unique high school course called "The American Woman." With her graduate degree in administration, she easily took to the role of president of the Concord teachers' union.

In 1984, President Reagan announced NASA's "Teacher in Space" program, "designed to inspire students, honor teachers and spur interest in mathematics, science and space exploration." Immediately—just as Sally Ride was years earlier when her opportunity beckoned—Christa McAuliffe was "all in."

No one who knew McAuliffe was surprised that she jumped at the chance to be a citizen-astronaut. It was a teacher's dream: the opportunity to take the ultimate field trip, to write the ultimate lesson plan. Quite simply, according to her obituary in *The New York Times*: "She hoped the program would help teaching, a profession that had come to need help."

McAuliffe was one of eleven thousand teacher-applicants, and in July 1985, among the ten who were chosen. She was assigned to the first "Teacher in Space" mission, scheduled for January 1986 aboard the shuttle *Challenger*. Leaving behind her husband and their young children in their New Hampshire home, she went to the NASA facility in Houston for extensive training, and much public attention.

How did Sally Ride know that she wanted to join NASA?

Many would assume that Dr. Ride's specialty of astrophysics—the study of how the universe (and everything in it) works—would lead naturally to a desire for a career in hands-on space exploration. Not necessarily, the field is rich in so many other possibilities. And not necessarily in the archaic times when there were few women in science, even fewer in physics. But her clear bent toward science in her education showed that there was fertile ground for the NASA seed to be planted. I'll say it again, though—interesting that no teacher, mentor, or advisor called the new NASA program to her attention. She herself saw the ball, grabbed it, and ran with it.

And what about . . . Shakespeare and a second BA, in English? Ride loved literature as much as she loved science. She found in Shakespeare's plays the same kind of intellectual challenge she found in science: solving puzzles. How do the dramatic plot points and characters knit together to make a whole? Clearly, Ride had the kind of mind that could see beyond the obvious, allowing her to grasp the opportunity that NASA presented.

Speaking of puzzles, another tantalizing clue to Ride's motivation can be found in tennis, a sport in which she excelled through high school and college, almost to the professional level. Stories conflict, but Billie Jean King, having played in an exhibition doubles' match with Sally in 1972, may have advised her to take up professional tennis; in any event, Sally was good enough that she could have had a formidable career. The clue here is the strength and athleticism necessary for such a career— plus the competitiveness, the pursuit of excellence, of mastery. These were key factors not only in Ride's character, but also among the reasons that NASA chose her.

I repeat, how did she know space flight was what she wanted to do? I think she was well-prepared for life and, with a secure base, she had the freedom and the confidence to leap into the unknown.

I'll ask the same question about Christa McAuliffe. How did she know that she wanted to join NASA? The "Teacher in Space" application asked the question directly: "Why do you want to be the first U.S. private citizen in space?" Her answer was one that so many other people—Ride included—could have made: the wonder of it all. McAuliffe wrote: "I remember the excitement in my home when the first satellites were launched. My parents were amazed, and I was caught up with their wonder . . . John F. Kennedy inspired me with his words about placing a man on the moon and I still remember a cloudy, raining night driving through Pennsylvania and hearing the news that the astronauts had landed safely."

Her obituary in *The New York Times* quotes a junior high school friend about McAuliffe's reaction to Shepard's "fifteen-minute suborbital hop" as follows: "She said to me that some-day she wanted to ride in space. We thought that by the time she finally would take the trip, it would be like an airplane ride."

Indeed, what did the *Challenger* and all the other STS shuttles look like? Airplanes that were designed to detach from the rockets that propelled them into space and, when their missions were complete, to glide back through the atmosphere to land on runways.

Excitement and amazement and wonder, however, were not all that motivated McAuliffe's desire for space travel. In her ap-plication to the "Teacher in Space" program, she—social stud-ies and history teacher to her core—showed how well she understood the priority of humanizing space flight. She cited the high school course she had developed as one of her selling points: "Just as the pioneer travelers of the Conestoga wagon days kept personal diaries, I, as a pioneer space traveler, would do the same. Future historians would use my eyewitness ac-counts to help in their studies of the impact of the Space Age on the general population."

And as an administrator who knew her way around educa-tional conferences, she committed herself to designing and car-rying out an extensive communications program after her mission, aimed squarely at educators and thus students: "The chance to . . . have a direct impact on education is an exciting prospect. The conference system of large audience lectures and small personal workshops would make it possible to reach many educators and thereby have a direct impact on students across the United States."

I wrote my master's thesis on NASA and its public information program. Of course, I had been fascinated as a young person by TV coverage of satellites and rockets and launches, of Neil Armstrong planting the American flag on the moon. I devoured press coverage of the astronauts and their families. Eventually I realized how important it was for our space agency to have a good reputation among the public, and what seemed to be fun for me to look at and read, was actually serious business. When I decided to make communications my career, it seemed natural for me to examine the mechanics of NASA's public information program. I assure you, that program was, and remains, nearly as complex and disciplined as everything else at NASA. My heart broke when one of the key elements of the program—live media coverage of launches—exposed the demise of the *Challenger* to thousands of people observing in person (including families of the astronauts) and millions on TV (including schoolchildren watching from their classrooms).

Christa McAuliffe was born in 1948, Sally Ride in 1951. Generationally, the three years that separated them is of no importance—they were part of the post-WWII Baby Boomer generation. They came of age in the 1960s and into the 1970s, a time of great social change in America.

Among the most profound of these changes was that the once widely accepted and age-old roles of girls and women were being re-examined and challenged. So many of these traditional roles had robbed girls and women of opportunities that boys and men enjoyed, or made them blind to their existence, or were the result of groundless assumptions. The "feminist movement" (or simply, "feminism") sought to change this particular status quo.

It is unfortunate that the words "feminist" and "feminism" became—and remain—so highly charged, with negative or militant overtones, taking the focus away from the true roles that women can choose and play out in their lives. Tantalizing questions can be asked about whether and how feminism inspired or allowed Christa and Sally to lead their lives the way they did.

Christa embraced the idea that she was free to design her own life. Very much a product of her time, she was immediately receptive to the feminist arguments that were advanced starting in the late 1960s. Even in opting to become a schoolteacher—a traditional occupation for women—she was, according to a high school classmate, choosing a career that would allow her to have it all as a wife, mother, and working professional.

Yet I detect a sense of longing for missed opportunities in the essay McAuliffe wrote as part of her application to the "Teacher in Space" program in 1985, years after Sally Ride had already "shattered [the] space ceiling," to use the words of *The New York Times*. The essay also conveyed a sense that she knew that her chosen life had given her a unique perspective that she could bring to NASA: "As a woman, I have been envious of those men who could participate in the space program . . . I cannot join the space program and restart my life as an astronaut, but this opportunity to connect my abilities as an educator with my interest in history and space is a unique opportunity to fulfill my early fantasies."

In 1972, in addition to the expansion of the astronaut program to a broader set of applicants, the military service academies in the United States began enrolling women and Title IX of the Education Amendments was passed by Congress to bar sex discrimination in education programs and activities offered by entities receiving federal financial assistance.

In the case of Sally Ride, did the nonexistence of Title IX during her high school and early college years change how she pursued her chosen sport—tennis—and whether she could/would/should have played it professionally? The answer is not clear, but I don't think so. Very little stopped her from playing tennis on a championship level for as long as she wanted to. She then seemed to make a reasoned choice to follow a path of education toward a future career, not athletics.

That path wended its way through science—physics specifically. Along the way, the young Sally received feminist encouragement at home, in elementary school, and in her single-sex high school.

For elucidation, I'll return to Lynn Sherr, a journalist who followed NASA among other subjects and ultimately became Sally Ride's friend. In her 2014 biography *Sally Ride*, Sherr wrote about the attitude of parents Joyce and Dale Ride toward their two daughters: "At a time when girls were supposed to get married, have a family and cook dinner every night in a kitchen with avocado-colored appliances, the Rides raised their daughters without preconceptions or gender restraints . . . and the gift of equality from both her parents helped guarantee Sally a boundless future."

The absence of "gender restraints" extended to Sally's favorite sport before she took up tennis—baseball, which she loved to play. Sherr wrote that she "revered the Los Angeles Dodgers . . . who became her personal obsession (she had boxes full of baseball cards) and an early thwarted career ambition. Playing shortstop for the Dodgers, Joyce would later say, was the only thing she told Sally she could not do simply because she was a girl."

Of Sally's experience in Los Angeles at the Westlake School for Girls (now co-ed and called Harvard-Westlake), Sherr reported: "Sally attributed much of her ability as an excellent student to being at a single-sex school. 'A lot of things that can kind of come into play when you're a 15-, 16-year-old girl with boys in the classroom just didn't happen at Westlake,' she said. 'I didn't succumb to the stereotype that science wasn't for girls.'"

Indeed, one of Sally's science teachers was "one of the few female PhDs in science . . . [who] brought her outrage over the unequal opportunities for women to her job at Westlake," wrote Sherr.

But as so many women know, Sally also heard other messages, sometimes from women such as another teacher who told her that she had a "first-rate mind, wasted in science" or a friend's mother who wondered, "Astrophysics? What are you ever going to do with that?" Even some of her friends were baffled by her love of science.

When Sally arrived at Stanford in 1970 as a transfer student from Swarthmore College, the discouraging messages continued, verbally and otherwise. There was only one woman majoring in physics at the time, and there was not even one woman on the physics faculty. The situation in the overall U.S. education system was not much different.

But these messages must not have been loud or strong enough to dissuade Sally. Even though, for the first time in her schooling, she encountered professors who disparaged female science students, she remained committed to the path she had chosen. As a friend said later, her view of succeeding in the world "was just to do it better than men or anyone else."

At the beginning of this chapter, I mentioned that Dr. Ride served on the boards of inquiry into the *Challenger* and *Columbia* disasters. Just a bit more detail on that aspect of her work for NASA.

The reports that resulted from both investigations found that systemic faults, within the culture and procedures of NASA and its suppliers, bore a large part of the blame for what had happened. The direct imputations against NASA, the agency that had fostered her, must have been especially painful; even so, she concurred with them. Ride was a clear-eyed scientist, looking at the evidence before her, the puzzle pieces falling into place with Shakespearean logic.

At the time of the *Challenger* inquiry, she was still a NASA employee. All along, she had intended to retire after her third mission—which never came—and return to academia. After the *Challenger* report was issued in June 1986, she was in fact on the verge of retirement, but was asked to take on a special strategic planning assignment. That yearlong effort produced what became known as the Ride Report—officially, "Leadership and America's Future in Space." Dr. Ride then retired, though she was called back from private life in 2003 for the *Columbia* inquiry.

The Ride Report was especially interesting to me for two prescient findings: (a) that NASA, with international cooperation, should explore planet Earth, our home, with rigor equal to that of space exploration and (b) the need for increased national attention to science education.

As regards finding (a)—how obvious yet how controversial, even with mounting and incontrovertible evidence of our plant's degradation. Using the NASA-speak of "mission," here's how the Ride Report framed the challenge: "NASA should embrace Mission to Planet Earth . . . Do we dare apply our capabilities to explore the mysteries of other worlds, and not also apply those capabilities to explore and understand the mysteries of our own world—mysteries which may have important implications for our future on this planet?"

And for finding (b), I envisioned Christa McAuliffe looking over Sally Ride's shoulder and nodding in affirmation. Eventually STEM would become the familiar acronym it is today.

Dr. Ride made such education the centerpiece of her life's work post-NASA and until her death in 2012 and even beyond, with her company Sally Ride Science (SRS). She founded SRS in 2001 with her life partner Tam O'Shaughnessy, who continues to run the not-for-profit (now based at UC San Diego) as executive director. The *mission* (yes, NASA-speak) continues: "to inspire young people in science, technology, engineering, and math (STEM) and to promote STEM literacy."

I will offer this epitaph for Sally Ride and Christa McAuliffe. It was written by journalist Lynn Sherr in the biography about her friend Sally, but I think it applies equally to each of these pioneering women: "Her life reminds us that whatever our own personal limits, there's something out there grander than we can measure, more marvelous than we can imagine; something just waiting to be explored."

22

STEVE JOBS
(United States)

AT AGE 25, STEVE JOBS WAS AT A HIGH POINT of his life. On December 12, 1980, Wall Street told him and the world that the company he had co-founded when he was 21, Apple, was valued at $1.778 billion.

"Going public"—Apple being listed as a public company and its stock beginning to trade on the NASDAQ exchange—had just put close to $300 million in his own pocket. Jobs was already a plain-vanilla millionaire based on the early pre–stock market success of Apple. The IPO, the largest since the Ford Motor Company IPO nearly a quarter-century earlier, boosted his status.

His "April" lasted five heady years, until he and his company stumbled. Jobs was forced out of Apple, into the "May" that Sinatra crooned about. He was still a multimillionaire and had lost none of his mojo, so he took his magic elsewhere, into new companies and new technologies. In Sinatra-speak: "I pick myself up and get back in the race."

And then it was "June"—well, actually it was December 1986. Jobs was "back on top," willing to accept an almost desperate invitation to return to a troubled Apple. He led for fifteen more years until his death.

Steve Jobs died on October 5, 2011. When that famous IPO

happened, he was halfway through his life. But his story did not die with him.

Apple, a pre-eminent "Big Tech" company, thrives, because of its products, its financial performance, and its value as an investment. Market capitalization today is $1.3 trillion. It is a major component of the Dow Jones Industrial Average and the Standard & Poor's index. It is number 4 on the Fortune 500 list of American companies, number 12 on the Global 500 list. All the normal markers of corporate success.

Through Apple, Steve Jobs changed the way we live. His legacy is still being formed and judged, a process that will continue for a long time to come. As examined a figure as he was during his life, as public as all his missteps and his accomplishments were, as much as he and Apple have been scrutinized—the story of Steve Jobs is still being written. And it is universally relevant; if it were not, nobody would care.

Assessing the impact of any person while they are alive is tricky. As Sinatra knew—and judging by the success of "That's Life," lots of fans resonated to that knowledge—you can veer from success to humiliation and back again like you're riding a pendulum or a seesaw. You can do something so embarrassing that you risk wiping out yourself and your reputation. The tenuousness of this situation is enhanced if you are a prominent person or a leader whose every move is tracked and analyzed, emulated and criticized. Jobs was such a person, such a leader.

Assessing his impact "only" ten years after his death is more than tricky; it is useless. Think of all the great leaders of the past, in every field, whose reputations and impact are still being measured. Time allows us to find new meaning in what these leaders did (or didn't do), as new information surfaces. The "papers" of U.S. presidents, for example, are typically sealed for a length of time, often decades, before they are made public. Time gives perspective.

Even so, there is already plenty on the record about Jobs, in portrayals appearing during his career and since his death. A lot of this output is contradictory, though it all purports to give the "real" and "true" story about an extraordinarily complex and even mysterious man. The process of assessing Steve Jobs is ongoing.

Some judgments don't need the test of time, though. As I consider Steve Jobs, I can't help thinking of the words attributed to Secretary of War Edwin Stanton as he stood at the deathbed of Abraham Lincoln, cut down, as we all know, by assassination just after the end of the Civil War—words that may well apply to Jobs: "Now he belongs to the ages."

Bare facts—and detailed analyses—of Jobs' personal and business life, his accomplishments and foibles, and so much else are well-known. Enter "Steve Jobs" in any search engine and start counting the references that appear. Then start reading and looking.

There are scores of books (including three in "graphic novel" style), probably thousands of articles and interviews, about a dozen feature films and documentaries. His story has been told in theater and opera, and through video. He is depicted as a character in a mural in Calais and as a bronze statue erected in a tech-oriented office park in Budapest just months after his death.

Steve Jobs was an inventor, an investor, an industrial designer, an entrepreneur, a magnate. He invented or transformed at least six industries:

- Personal computing
- Tablet computing
- Animated movies
- Digital publishing
- Music distribution
- Phones

And if "popular culture" is an industry, add it to the list!

Just a brief recap of his early life will set the scene. Steve Jobs was born February 24, 1955, in San Francisco. Adopted as an infant by Clara and Paul Jobs, who later also adopted a daughter, Patricia. Raised in a middle-class environment in what we now know as Silicon Valley, just as it was becoming a super-heated technology capital. Graduated from Homestead High School in Los Altos in 1972. Went to Reed College in Oregon for one semester and dropped out. Started tinkering on various inventions in his parents' garage with some buddies . . . and voilà . . . Apple emerged.

A more nuanced look at his early biography shows us that young Steve's school years were marked by curiosity, independence, and a certain amount of turmoil. Clara had taught him to read early, and when schooltime arrived he was easily bored in classrooms and became known as a prankster. Steve skipped the fifth grade (his teacher wanted him to skip two grades, but his parents objected), which made him young among his peers. By age 10, his interest in electronics and engineering and invention was obvious. He lived and breathed in Silicon Valley, a rapidly developing technology capital full of computer scientists and engineers and inventors. At home, he had the example of Paul, a machinist most of his life, who taught his son how to build things and who defended him to at least one doubting teacher as "brilliant."

The early years led to an adolescence and young adulthood marked by experiments and explorations, searches for all sorts of meaning, missteps, independent learning. Marked by innovation, creativity, talent, and curiosity. A routine defiance of others' expectations. An ironclad belief in himself and what he was doing. He came to see himself as ahead of the game and determined to stay there. His parents and teachers and friends and family and colleagues saw all this.

And then he and his friends Steve Wozniak and Ron Wayne made Apple.

★   ★   ★

Yes, in 1980 at age 25, Steve Jobs was a self-made millionaire many times over. That fact merely described the man then and would hold for the rest of his life. I'm more interested in this: What *defined* the man? Trying to answer that question is, in my opinion, what really counts for readers of this book. Few of us will ever be in Jobs's financial position at any age, but all of us can be inspired by what Jobs brought to his life and his work.

A complex man such as Steve Jobs can be defined in many ways. First, perhaps foremost, he was a person who made the most of his individuality. As a child, as a young person, in the pre-IPO days and after, for his entire life. Each one of us possesses individuality—but do we care, do we *dare*, to make the most of it? This is the inspiration I take from looking at Steve Jobs at age 25.

Thinking about individuality leads me to think about being unique, another way to define Jobs. Of course, every single human being is a unique collection of strengths and weaknesses. Even identical twins develop uniquely. I'm not saying anything original; we all know that. But are we willing to *live* as if we know it? This question must be front-and-center for each of us. Along with its answer, it can be called our North Star, that's how important they both are.

I think the answer Jobs gave was—"Yes, I'm willing." I am not sure we all would say that. His willingness guaranteed that his unique individuality would have an effect beyond himself. His individuality transformed into ideas that have changed the world. Into technologies that have redefined technology. Into products that have captivated millions of people.

Another defining characteristic that Jobs possessed was self-confidence. He had it before all that IPO money arrived. Maybe he was born with it. It was woven into his entire life.

Self-confidence has many downsides. It can be cocky. It can be difficult to live or work with. It can mean "me first, you never." It can be married to self-absorption, or self-centeredness, or arbitrary behavior, or put-downs of others, or a lack of connection with others—any number of psychological displays.

And it's not for me to say: That judgment is a private one reserved for his family and colleagues. What I can say is that self-confidence was fuel for his vision and a major factor in Jobs's success.

Looking from the outside and judging him by his actions, I offer this overarching defining trait, one visible to all: that Jobs approached his life and his work with passion.

"Passion" is a very charged word. Synonyms for "passion"—fervor, intensity, enthusiasm, eagerness, zeal, vehemence, vigor, avidity, feeling, emotion, fierceness, excitement, energy, animation, gusto, zest, spirit, commitment. Also—fury, frenzy, fever, mania, obsession, lust, temper.

Clues to the value Jobs placed on the foundational role of "passion" can be found in his own words. Speaking at the "All Things Digital" conference in May 2007, he said, "People say you have to have a lot of passion for what you're doing, and it's totally true. And the reason is because it's so hard that if you don't, any rational person would give up."

And speaking at the Stanford University Commencement on June 12, 2005, he said, "Your work is going to fill a large part of your life, and the only way to be truly satisfied is to do what you believe is great work. And the only way to do great work is to love what you do. Don't settle."

At 25, Steve Jobs had achieved a level of success others would have rested on at age 50. That, of course, was almost all the time he'd have. He made the most of every day. Will you?

23

JEAN-MICHEL BASQUIAT
(United States)

WELL ON HIS WAY TO FAME AND ACHIEVEMENT by the time he was 21 in 1981, the year when he came to the attention of the New York art world. Dead in 1988 from a heroin overdose. This was Jean-Michel Basquiat, the avant-garde Brooklyn-born Black painter whose highly personal yet universal work continues to occupy a singular place in the canon of twentieth-century art and whose impact remains strong.

Any such death leaves at least one question in its aftermath: "Why?" And when the person is young and talented and visionary and already tasting success, there can be another question: "Wasn't it enough?" And, poignantly, "What would he have gone on to do?"

The artist Keith Haring, friend and peer, eulogized Jean-Michel Basquiat in *Vogue*. Was he thinking beyond just one young man's legacy? Haring, who was at the same point in his own blossoming career, would be taken the next year by AIDS. Consider these words that could apply to so many: "Greedily we wonder what masterpieces we might have been cheated out of by his death . . . only now will people begin to understand the magnitude of his contribution."

Jean-Michel Basquiat embarked on his blazing artistic path

when he was very, very young. Even before he was school age, his abilities were noted and encouraged. It seems that he always knew what he wanted to do in his life—make art from, and about, every single thing that came his way. Visual art mostly, but also music and writing. He wanted to get famous and make money, too, because he was ambitious. He made art and money, until he couldn't. He has remained famous. And more than one observer has blamed fame as much as drugs for his death. *A Quick Killing in Art* is the title of just one of his biographies.

The second child of a Haitian immigrant father and an American mother of Puerto Rican descent, Jean-Michel was born on December 22, 1960. His older brother had just died; he would eventually have two younger sisters. His fatal overdose was on August 12, 1988.

Knowing what you want to do and actually doing it are two very different things. In some people, that procession can take years. Not so in Jean-Michel's case. Precociously reading and writing by age 4; drawing cartoons on paper that his accountant father brought home from the office; being taken to New York's art museums and the theater by his mother at an early age; attending an art-oriented elementary school in Brooklyn; writing his first book at age 7; soaking up everything that his urban, multicultural environment presented—these were among the influences that set him on his unique path. Years later, he would define "influence" as "someone's idea going through my new mind."

Basquiat's "new mind" would lead him as a teenager first to graffiti art and, ultimately, to *sui generis* collages and paintings that art critics described as prime examples of Neo-Expressionism. This art movement emerged worldwide in the late 1970s and began hitting its stride in the early 1980s, just as Basquiat himself was emerging and hitting his stride.

Neo-Expressionism was a major art movement in Europe and the United States during the 1980s. The young artists who dominated the movement turned away from Abstract Expressionism and returned to portraying the human body and other recognizable objects, but in uniquely expressive ways. And as britannica.com described it, "The movement was linked to and in part generated by new and aggressive methods of salesmanship, media promotion, and marketing on the part of dealers and galleries."

Jean-Michel Basquiat's brief life did not keep him from scaling the heights of accomplishment. But his path was not easy or smooth as a child or as an adolescent; drugs, fame, and money would complicate his brief young adulthood.

At age 7, he was hit by a car and severely injured. To help soothe him during a long recuperation, his mother gave him a copy of the medical reference book *Gray's Anatomy*. An unusual way to divert a child! The combination of *Gray's Anatomy* text and detailed drawings intrigued Jean-Michel and showed up stylistically in his artwork; in his late teens, he formed an experimental musical band with his friend Michael Holman called Gray.

Soon after the accident, his parents separated, and his father began raising the three children. They lived in Brooklyn until 1974, then moved to Puerto Rico for a few years. Upon their return to Brooklyn, life broke apart in many ways. His mother's mental instability had long been evident, and she was committed to a treatment facility. The resulting family instability became unavoidable. Jean-Michel ran away from home to live in Washington Square Park; he later said of that period: "I just sat there dropping acid for eight months." He eventually returned to his father and his sisters, but his situation continued to deteriorate. His father was a known womanizer. He was rough on his son. This intelligent student, skilled in art, writing, music, and languages (because of his parentage, he was fluent in three), failed in conventional school. He was either expelled from or dropped out of even an alternative high school by age 17. This time around, he didn't need to run away from home—his father kicked him out.

Jean-Michel may have failed in school, but he was soon successful at attracting attention for his art. Operating from a downtown Manhattan tenement that was run-down even for a tenement (or from a park bench when he was homeless), he began practicing the foundation of all his work: graffiti or street art . . . or vandalism, depending on your point of view.

> If you've ever had to scrub off any d*** spray-painted markings from the walls of your building, you probably regard graffiti as vandalism, probably gang-related. The *Britannica* encyclopedia calls it a "form of visual communication, usually illegal, involving the unauthorized marking of public space by an individual or group." There was nothing gang-related about SAMO; personal expression was everything. Yet I do wonder who cleaned up those walls and streets?

Along with his friend Al Diaz, Basquiat invented the tag SAMO (which usually included the *copyright icon*, seemingly just for fun). SAMO was an utterly idiosyncratic combination of scribbled symbols and sarcastic slogans that added up to a form of social criticism—"a tool for mocking bogusness," he later said. The tag was ubiquitous on mostly downtown streets and the walls of commercial buildings, but anonymous; this added to its allure, with the *SoHo News* asking "Whose?" and the *Village Voice*, "Boosh-Wah or CIA?"

SAMO's origin story, according to the Los Angeles museum The Broad, is this: "In the late 1970s, brief, cryptic messages began to appear on the streets of Manhattan, all signed SAMO.

These subversive, sometimes menacing statements . . . piqued the curiosity of viewers around New York and soon gained notoriety in the art world."

Art critic Jeffrey Deitch, who called it "disjoined street poetry," said, "You couldn't go anywhere interesting in Lower Manhattan without noticing that someone named SAMO had been there first." One Basquiat biographer noted that "while some of the phrases might seem political, none of them were simple propaganda slogans. Some were outright surrealist or looked like fragments of poetry."

SAMO "broke up" around 1980 ("SAMO is dead" epitaphs started appearing around the city), about the same time that Keith Haring figured out that his new friend Jean-Michel was behind the activity. Soon Jean-Michel would be anonymous no more, but not quite yet.

He first fell in with a group of social activist artists who decided to "show their stuff" in what today we might call a "pop-up" setting. According to The Broad, "A wall covered with the spray paint and brushwork of SAMO received favorable notices in the press."

That "wall" was actually a mural, the first piece of indoor art that Basquiat ever showed publicly; it was June 1980, and he was still using the SAMO tag. The show came to the attention of the publication *Art in America*, where critic Jeffrey Deitch singled out "a patch of wall painted by SAMO, the omnipresent graffiti sloganeer . . . a knockout combination of de Kooning and subway paint scribbles."

This was the beginning of the art world's discovery of Jean-Michel Basquiat, the end of anonymity. Choose your cliché to describe what began happening to Jean-Michel as he gained increasing attention from critics and agents and journalists and collectors: "snowballing . . . runaway freight train . . . like a shooting star . . . meteoric rise . . . in the spotlight." Every name associated with "art" would soon covet his work.

★   ★   ★

Fast-forward to February 1981, when twenty of Basquiat's paintings (signed with his own name) were in a show of one hundred "New York/New Wave" artists that the prominent dealer Annina Nosei visited. She was smitten with Basquiat but stunned to learn that he had no inventory beyond what was in the show. "You don't have *anything*?" She asked him, according to Stephen Metcalfe writing in *The Atlantic*. And so Nosei did something remarkable: she turned over the basement of her Prince Street gallery to Basquiat so he could begin producing paintings for her to sell upstairs. "His work [began] to mature so quickly, so decisively, one can scarcely process it," Metcalfe reported.

After a month working frantically in the gallery's basement, Jean-Michel was in a group show in the gallery. His six paintings sold easily, which gave Nosei another idea. She set him up in a studio-loft where he could live and work. She supplied the paint, brushes, and canvases he needed and even provided assistants to work with him. As the paintings emerged, she of course was the one to sell them, and there were plenty of collectors waiting to buy. "Basquiat," Metcalfe said, "had arrived."

Indeed he had, for Jean-Michel Basquiat exploded onto the art world stage. Many shows, patrons, collectors—and paintings rushed to market almost directly from his brush before they were dry—lay ahead. His personal way of expressing himself would coalesce with a worldwide movement. He would be mentioned in the same breath as every important artist of the twentieth century, worldwide.

If you're keeping track, you know that he had only a few more years to live. He didn't know that, but I wonder if it would have changed the way he lived and painted.

In the brief time left to him, he hit and then crested the wave of notoriety and critical acclaim and financial success. Danger was already lurking for this artist to whom street drugs of all sorts were not an unknown. As noted by Metcalfe in *The Atlantic*: "Basquiat had arrived, but he, at least, didn't seem sure where."

★   ★   ★

On Sunday, February 10, 1985, Jean-Michel Basquiat received the imprimatur of the *New York Times Magazine,* which featured him as the centerpiece of its cover story, "New Art, New Money: The Marketing of an American Artist" by Cathleen McGuigan.

The story spotlighted Basquiat as a celebrity because that's what he was, and that was the culture of the 1980s. He stood at the center of a wide and multi-lane intersection awash, indeed flooded, with art, artists, agents, critics, high finance, talent, promotion, notoriety, clients . . . with drug use a constant in his days. Even so, he was held out as the exemplar of the explosive art market in the latter part of the twentieth century. It would be hard to overstate the impact of McGuigan's account of how Basquiat had gotten to the pinnacle he then occupied. "The nature and rapidity of his climb is unimaginable in another era," she wrote.

But what did his work *look* like? Imagine graphite, colored pencil, oil stick, acrylic paints, watercolor, torn and pasted paper . . . all coalescing into a reality that transcended his graffiti roots. Imagine *energy.* Wrote McGuigan: "His color-drenched canvases are peopled with primitive figures wearing menacing masklike faces, painted against fields jammed with arrows, grids, crowns, skyscrapers, rockets and words." His *paintings,* she said, balance "seemingly contradictory forces: control and spontaneity, menace and wit, urban imagery and primitivism."

From my vantage point today, the *Times* story seems very fresh. Basquiat would be dead three years later, yet in death his work has only grown in renown. Young artists continue to emerge with back stories just as unique, in their own way, as Basquiat's. The art market of the early twenty-first century is even more of a hothouse, with the celebrity, personal, and financial stakes even higher.

I want to return to Annina Nosei and her patronage of Basquiat. She was not alone in flocking to Basquiat. In many ways, she represented the entire system of agents, dealers, critics, journalists, and others that exists to support artists, a system that certainly benefited Basquiat. Everything written about Basquiat, then and now, is replete with the names of people indispensable in this system. But I find her specific story illuminating.

I can't shake how problematic the unorthodox gallery basement setup seemed. Yes, it kick-started the career of Nosei's newly discovered artist. But as critic Suzi Gablik said in the *Times* story, it was "something like a hothouse for forced growth." The story also quoted Jeffrey Deitch from a review in his magazine *Flash Art*: "Basquiat is likened to a wild boy raised by wolves, corralled into Annina's basement and given nice clean canvases to work on."

Thinking about this problematic setup leads me to another aspect of Basquiat's story: the centrality of race and racial identity in his oeuvre. As Metcalfe wrote in *The Atlantic*: "The [Nosei gallery] arrangement understandably makes commentators squirm: A White taskmistress keeping a Black ward in her basement to turn out paintings on command."

How did Basquiat view the situation? His words seem to indicate that he shrugged it off, even as his work began moving more obviously to racial themes. *The Atlantic*: "Basquiat himself said, 'That [taskmistress comment] has a nasty edge to it, you know. I was never locked anywhere. If I was White, they would just say 'artist in residence.' At the same time, race enters his work more explicitly."

He told Cathleen McGuigan for the *Times* story: "The Black person is the protagonist in most of my paintings. I realized that I didn't see many paintings with Black people in them."

Let's focus on the racial explicitness of just one of his works: "Defacement (The Death of Michael Stewart)." Made in 1983, this work is a precursor emblem of the Black Lives Matter movement. It is its own microcosm of how Basquiat absorbed the world and then made manifest his reaction to the world via his personal iconography. "Defacement" is as relevant today as it was the day it was painted—actually, drawn with markers onto a wall in Keith Haring's studio, another mural.

Michael Stewart was a young Black graffiti artist who was arrested by NYC transit police because he was tagging in a subway station. Tied up with zip-ties, screaming, "What did I do? What did I do?" and beaten into a coma, he died thirteen days later. (The eleven transit police involved were acquitted two years later of various charges.) Basquiat, who knew Stewart, was gravely affected by the brutality of the event.

"Defacement" is replete with symbolism. The word itself is scrawled in capital letters near the top edge of the work, above a star and just under "C. O. P.," with other scratchy letter-like marks nearby. The word is punctuated with Spanish-language-style question marks, the second "e" is scratched out, and the *copyright icon* follows the word. Floating on a mostly white field amidst patches of black and blue and maroon are two blue-uniformed figures with menacing maroon faces. The figures are wearing official-looking caps with yellow stars and wielding nightsticks. They are beating a figure that appears only as a full-length black silhouetted body with what seems to be a crown of thorns on its head.

The word "defacement" has multiple meanings. It is a term for graffiti because graffiti defaces surfaces. And Basquiat defaced the word even as he used it. Its synonyms relate to mutilating, spoiling, marring, disfiguring, rendering invalid. Defacing a person is a crime. Basquiat is asking whether the killing of the young Black man—crowned as Jesus was on the cross—is a crime.

"Defacement" stayed where Basquiat put it—on the studio wall—for two years. Then Haring cut it out from the wall, framed it like a classic "masterpiece" (gilded frame and all), and hung it over his bed. It was there at the time of his death.

It is now owned by Haring's goddaughter, who has lent it to museums very occasionally. Its most recent viewing was at the Guggenheim in the summer of 2019.

The tragedy of any life cut short by drugs is undeniable. In the case of Jean-Michel Basquiat, whose artistic output cannot be separated from his drug use, many ways remain to transcend the tragedy and appreciate his impact. You need only to put his name into your search engine and revel in his images, his reviews, his biography.

Here are two looks at his continuing impact.

First, the astonishing amounts of money that his paintings now command. The 2016 sale at auction (Christie's) of *Untitled* (depicting a devil) for $57.3 million broke the American record. The 2017 sale at auction (Sotheby's) of *Untitled* (depicting a skull) for $110.5 million broke the American record again. Both works were purchased by the same man: Japanese billionaire fashion entrepreneur Yusaku Maezawa, who pledged that the works would remain available for the public to view, in the museum that (as of September 2021) he was planning to build in his hometown of Chiba.

Speaking specifically of the $110.5 million *Untitled*, he said: "When I first encountered this painting, I was struck with so much excitement and gratitude for my love of art. I want to share that experience with as many people as possible. I hope it brings as much joy to others as it does to me."

The painting has been on a world tour that started in 2019 at the Brooklyn Art Museum (where his mother long ago bought Basquiat a junior membership).

Second, his regular-guy profile. Go to NetDaily.com, the "fan pages" of the NBA's Brooklyn Nets. There you can learn about the Basquiat-inspired jersey for the team's 2020–2021 season. The Nets star forward Kevin Durant, himself a major fan of the artist, was instrumental in getting Basquiat's distinctive imagery included in the NBA's "City Editions" line of jerseys.

Durant is known for studying leaders in all fields. As he says it, "how they got to that point, mastering their craft . . . I just try to see what their perspective was and try to make it my own and do my own thing."

Sounds a bit like Jean-Michel Basquiat's definition of influence, which I cited earlier: "Someone's idea going through my new mind."

EPILOGUE

So THERE YOU HAVE IT: twenty-five men and women who used a variety of strategies to rise out of difficult personal circumstances, overcome great obstacles, defy their critics, and attain success—in other words, to "nail it."

In almost every case these men and women took prudent risks, were oblivious to criticism, and exercised a laser-like focus on their objectives.

Remember EDITH PIAF, who was abandoned as a child, grew up under the most devastating of circumstances, but poured her heart and soul into her singing and became an international star.

Take inspiration from JACKIE ROBINSON, who was called upon to break through a seemingly impenetrable racial barrier and, on the advice of his mentor, BRANCH RICKEY, kept his cool in the face of taunts and threats to make history.

Think of ROBERTO MARINHO, who, while still in his early twenties, had enormous expectations thrust upon him as the heir to his father's business but showed the patience and determination to learn his craft and rose to a position of national influence.

Look to MAYA ANGELOU, who endured hardships and dislocations in her childhood and was abused and raped as a teenager, but found the spirit to turn her sufferings into prose and poetry that moved the nation.

Can you do the kind of things they did? Can you, like them, measure up to the challenges you face and achieve the goals that will make your life what you want it to be?

Of course you can! Just set your objective and think in specific terms about what it will take to get there. Then stay on track. Put every distraction and temptation aside no matter how attractive it be at the time.

Is there a benefit to doing this? You bet there is. The world is full of timid souls and idle dreamers who never really go after what they want. Don't be one of them. Work to stand out and use the lessons you've learned from this book. If you take that approach and stick with it, it will change your life for the better.

Now, go out there and *nail it*.

ACKNOWLEDGMENTS

This book would not be possible without the thoughtful research and writing and editing of Susan Black, a professional with remarkable talent. Ms. Black has developed every chapter. Special thanks to Joan Avagliano, also an individual of remarkable talent. It has been my privilege to work with Ms. Black and Ms. Avagliano for more than thirty years.

Robert Laird, whom I have worked for nearly twenty years and to whom this book is dedicated, did a masterful job bringing the entire book into focus.

My wife, Jan, a painter of some caliber who took time from this pursuit to help encourage me and to offer advice on nearly every individual treated, deserves high praise.

Michaela Hamilton, executive editor at Kensington, the female Maxwell Perkins, is a great champion and supporter of good writing, and it is a privilege to work with her. Special thanks to the staff of the Canby Public Library in Canby, Oregon; Anthony F. Quiles-Roche, who works tirelessly to raise the bar for all around him; Francine Benedetti and Nataliya Lustig, who helped keep me on track to complete the project.

So many friends who brought individuals to my attention that clearly set a path in their early days and made a mark on the world, including Rainer Gut, Angela Riley, Scott Freidheim, Kiera Parrott, Brian Moran, Marcy Syms, Lee Miringoff, Joe Wright, Saundra Cowen, Catherine Kinney, Ernie Anastos, Leora Levy, Lee Miringoff, and Phillip Muhr.

Of course, my family gave me the inspiration and conviction to write and finish this book: my sons, Geoffrey and Peter; my brother, Jack; my sisters, Mary Shay and Martha Doughty.

INDEX